C-3940

CAREER EXAMINATION SERIES

THIS IS YOUR **PASSBOOK®** FOR ...

TRANSPORTATION SECURITY SCREENER

NATIONAL LEARNING CORPORATION®
passbooks.com

PASSBOOK® SERIES

THE *PASSBOOK® SERIES* has been created to prepare applicants and candidates for the ultimate academic battlefield – the examination room.

At some time in our lives, each and every one of us may be required to take an examination – for validation, matriculation, admission, qualification, registration, certification, or licensure.

Based on the assumption that every applicant or candidate has met the basic formal educational standards, has taken the required number of courses, and read the necessary texts, the *PASSBOOK® SERIES* furnishes the one special preparation which may assure passing with confidence, instead of failing with insecurity. Examination questions – together with answers – are furnished as the basic vehicle for study so that the mysteries of the examination and its compounding difficulties may be eliminated or diminished by a sure method.

This book is meant to help you pass your examination provided that you qualify and are serious in your objective.

The entire field is reviewed through the huge store of content information which is succinctly presented through a provocative and challenging approach – the question-and-answer method.

A climate of success is established by furnishing the correct answers at the end of each test.

You soon learn to recognize types of questions, forms of questions, and patterns of questioning. You may even begin to anticipate expected outcomes.

You perceive that many questions are repeated or adapted so that you can gain acute insights, which may enable you to score many sure points.

You learn how to confront new questions, or types of questions, and to attack them confidently and work out the correct answers.

You note objectives and emphases, and recognize pitfalls and dangers, so that you may make positive educational adjustments.

Moreover, you are kept fully informed in relation to new concepts, methods, practices, and directions in the field.

You discover that you arre actually taking the examination all the time: you are preparing for the examination by "taking" an examination, not by reading extraneous and/or supererogatory textbooks.

In short, this PASSBOOK®, used directedly, should be an important factor in helping you to pass your test.

TRANSPORTATION SECURITY SCREENER
SUPERVISORY TRANSPORTATION SECURITY SCREENER

INTRODUCTION

INFORMATION FOR APPLICANTS INTERESTED IN APPLYING FOR:
· SCREENER WORKFORCE ACTION TEAM MEMBER (SWAT) ·
· SUPERVISORY TRANSPORTATION SECURITY SCREENER (STSS) ·
· TRANSPORTATION SECURITY SCREENER (TSS) ·

SCREENER WORKFORCE ACTION TEAM MEMBERS (SWAT)

What will I do as a Screener Workforce Action Team member?

SWAT members are Supervisory Transportation Security Screeners. You will fill personnel gaps created by the short-term loss of contract screeners. While deployed, you may serve as either a supervisor or TSS, depending on what is needed. You will remain on site until permanent TSSs are deployed. As a SWAT member, you will gain valuable knowledge and understanding of how the screening operation works, in all airport categories and in many locations. Your experience will be invaluable in assisting the airport management team with operational issues and in mentoring, coaching and training new TSSs.

You will be required to sign a one-year mobility agreement saying you are willing and available to travel from airport to airport during the year.

When your permanent duty location airport is completely converted, you will be one of the federal Transportation Security Screener Supervisors. At this point, your term as a SWAT member will terminate, and you will cease to be deployed.

Upon completion of your duties as a SWAT member, you will be permanently located at the airport you choose as your permanent duty station.

TSA will be recruiting additional SWATs to fill in behind SWATs who are no longer mobile, as their permanent airport has been totally converted from contract screeners to TSS or as SWAT members leave for other reasons.

If I am hired as a Supervisor and serve as a member of the Screener Workforce Action Team (SWAT), will my pay rate change?

No. As long as you are officially employed as a Supervisor, your pay rate will not be reduced, even if you are asked to serve in the capacity of a screener.

What does "one year mobility agreement" mean?

As a SWAT member, you will be required to travel from airport to airport for approximately a one-year period. Because we cannot anticipate where you may be needed at this time, you will be required to sign the mobility agreement so that we may deploy you to airport locations as needed. You will be paid standard government travel and per diem in addition to your salary.

This announcement requires people to travel. I cannot travel. Is this the only chance I will get to apply for federal Transportation Security Screener positions?

No, this announcement is for mobile Transportation Security Screener positions (SWAT members). Local job openings for federal Transportation Security Screener positions (both supervisory and screener) for each airport in the U.S. and its territories will be posted at later times. These future openings will be posted at www.tsa.gov as the process continues, and you should check back frequently.

QUESTIONS ABOUT SUPERVISORY TRANSPORTATION SECURITY SCREENERS

As a Supervisory Transportation Security Screener, what will I do?

As a Supervisory Transportation Security Screener:

You will coach, manage and ensure the performance and training of personnel that provide the front-line security and protection of air travelers, airplanes and airports. This frontline defense is responsible for:
Identifying dangerous or deadly objects in baggage, cargo and on passengers and preventing those objects from being transported onto the aircraft.
Performing this security mission in a courteous and professional manner.
You will supervise the members of your staff who will use diverse, cutting-edge electronic detection and imaging equipment;
At some point, you may participate in or attend meetings where classified information is provided.

As a Supervisory Transportation Security Screener (STSS), how much money will I make?

The basic salary range is from $36,400 to $56,400 a year depending upon your qualifications and experience. In addition to the basic pay for this position, you will receive extra pay, called locality pay, and based on the geographic area of your permanent duty station, which helps to positively adjust your salary for cost of living.
If you are a STSS SWAT member, while deployed, you will receive travel and per diem pay in addition to your salary.
The Federal Government offers generous benefits including Life Insurance, Health Insurance and Retirement Programs. These benefits are partially paid by the Federal Government. You will also earn vacation time and sick leave.

QUESTIONS ABOUT TRANSPORTATION SECURITY SCREENERS

As a Transportation Security Screener, what will I do?

You will provide front-line security and protection of air travelers, airports and airplanes. As the front-line defense, you are responsible for identifying dangerous or deadly objects in baggage, cargo and on passengers and preventing those objects from being transported onto aircraft. In ensuring the identification of dangerous or deadly objects in baggage, cargo, or on an air traveler, you must perform this essential security mission in a courteous and professional manner. You will use diverse, cutting-edge, electronic detection and imaging equipment. Finally, you may participate in or attend meetings where classified information is provided.

As a Transportation Security Screener, how much money will I make?

The basic salary range is from $25,140 to $43,350 a year depending upon your qualifications and experience. In addition to the basic pay for this position, you will receive extra pay, called locality pay, and based on the geographic area of your permanent duty station, which helps to positively adjust your salary for cost of living.

The Federal Government offers generous benefits including Life Insurance, Health Insurance and Retirement Programs. These benefits are partially paid by the Federal Government. You will also earn vacation time and sick leave.

As a Transportation Security Screener, can I earn more than the base salary of $43,350 a year?

No, not initially. However, this is a career position that offers you promotion potential.

When will you be hiring for airports in my location?

Check the Transportation Security Administration's website — www.tsa.gov — to find out when future hiring will take place for Transportation Security Screeners. Information about hiring in.your local area will be provided by radio, local TV, and local press.

If I want to apply to an airport outside of where I live, will you pay my moving expenses?

No. Our initial hiring focus is to fill the local airport(s) TSS positions with local residents.

Can I work part-time?

Depending upon specific work requirements, some airports may hire part-time TSSs.

What will my work schedule be?

Your supervisor will determine your work schedule. However, to be considered for employment you *must* be able to irregular hours and/or shifts, holidays and weekends, overtime, and beyond eight hours a day, if required.

QUESTIONS REGARDING ALL POSITIONS

Am I qualified to be a Transportation Security Screener?

Basic requirements:

> You must be a United States citizen, AND you must have one of the following:
> - High school diploma; or
> - General education diploma; or
> - At least one year of full-time work experience in security work or aviation screener work, or with x-ray technician work.

> In addition, in accordance with Public Law 107-71, you will be required to pass the following:

> - Transportation Security Screener aptitude test
> - English language proficiency test
> - Background check
> - Medical and physical examination
> - Pre-employment drug test

> Supervisory positions require additional experience and qualifications.

How do I apply?

> Screener vacancies will be posted at various times and individuals will be able to apply online at the TSA website. Check the site at www.tsa.gov for current employment opportunities.

I got the notification that says I meet the basic qualifications. Do I get the job?

> Not necessarily. Your application will be evaluated for your qualifications, experience, hiring preference, and how your qualifications compare to other candidates. You may be referred to an assessment center for additional evaluation. The series of assessments will include the tests and checks mentioned above, in addition to an interview.
> TSA will apply Title V veterans preference. Also, the law established an additional veterans preference as follows:

VETERANS PREFERENCE: The Under Secretary shall provide a preference for the hiring of an individual as a security screener if the individual is a member or former member of the armed forces and if the individual is entitled, under statute, to retired, retirement or retainer pay on account of service as a member of the armed forces.

> Further, the Secretary of Transportation and the Under Secretary committed to provide preference to displaced airline employees in filling the TSS positions.

Why must you administer these assessments?

Public Law 107-71. which requires the Federal Government to assume management of TSS duties, mandates that the government administer the above-listed assessments. These additional requirements are measured at Assessment Centers.

Where are Assessment Centers located?

Assessment Centers will be located close to local airports. For the STSSs who will be a part of the SWAT, we will provide air travel and lodging, if required, to one of our two to three national assessment centers.

Will I be notified to go to an Assessment Center?

Whether you are contacted and asked to come to an Assessment Center depends on the number of applicants, the number of people we are hiring, your qualifications, experience and hiring preference. If you receive notification, it will be either by phone from the Assessment Center Scheduler, or via e-mail with notification information.

I passed the assessments. Do I have the job?

Not necessarily. Once you have passed all the assessments, you are eligible for hire. Actual hiring decisions are based on local airport requirements and the number of eligible candidates.

Do I get paid for time spent completing the assessments?

No.

What happens after I am offered the job?

If offered the job, you will be conditionally employed until you:

- successfully complete 40 hours of classroom training;
- successfully complete 60 hours of on-the-job training; AND
- pass the certification examination.

Should I reapply?

Your application is good for one year, and you should not reapply during this period unless you receive additional training, education or experience related to TSS work. We may contact you at any time during this period if we need additional candidates at your airport.

What do I do if I'm confused about a specific question on the questionnaire?

Please answer all questions to the best of your ability. We are unable to assist you in answering questions.

I was in the middle of completing my application, and it was interrupted. What do I do?

You may re-enter the system and will need to re-enter your Social Security Number. You will need to start the questionnaire from the beginning.

How long will it take me to apply?

We anticipate that it will take applicants approximately 30 minutes to complete the application, and approximately 1-2 days to complete the assessment process.

Why do I have to meet all of these security requirements? (Drug screening, background check, etc.)

Due to the sensitive nature of this work, the Aviation and Transportation Security Act (ATSA) require that these security requirements be met.

How do I demonstrate that I am a displaced airline employee?

A displaced airline employee is someone who lost his or her airline job after September 11, 2001. On the questionnaire, you will be given the opportunity to indicate that you are a displaced airline employee under this definition. If you are asked to come to an Assessment center, you will need to bring evidence such as pay slips, letter of termination. etc. If you need assistance, please contact your previous employer.

PUBLIC LAW 107-71
SEC. 111. TRAINING AND EMPLOYMENT OF SECURITY SCREENING PERSONNEL

(a) IN GENERAL- Section 44935 of title 49, United States Code, is amended —
    (1) by redesignating subsection (f) as subsection (i); and
    (2) by striking subsection (e) and inserting the following;
(e) SECURITY SCREENERS-
    (1) TRAINING PROGRAM- The Under Secretary of Transportation for Security shall establish a program for the hiring and training of security screening personnel.
    (2) HIRING-
(A) QUALIFICATIONS- Within 30 days after the date of enactment of the Aviation and Transportation Security Act, the Under Secretary shall establish qualification standards for individuals to be hired by the United States as security screening personnel. Notwithstanding any provision of law, those standards shall require, at a minimum, an individual—
        (i)   to have a satisfactory or better score on a Federal security screening personnel selection examination;
        (ii)   to be a citizen of the United States;
        (iii)   to meet, at a minimum, the requirements set forth in subsection (f);

      (iv)   to meet such other qualifications as the Under Secretary may establish; and

      (v)   to have the ability to demonstrate daily a fitness for duty without any impairment due to illegal drugs, sleep deprivation, medication, or alcohol.

(B) BACKGROUND CHECKS- The Under Secretary shall require that an individual to be hired as a security screener undergo an employment investigation (including a criminal history record check) under section 44936(a)(1)

(C) DISQUALIFICATION OF INDIVIDUALS WHO PRESENT NATIONAL SECURITY RISKS- The Under Secretary, in consultation with the heads of other appropriate Federal agencies, shall establish procedures, in addition to any background check conducted under section 44936, to ensure that no individual who presents a threat to national security is employed as a security screener.

(3) EXAMINATION; REVIEW OF EXISTING RULES- The Under Secretary shall develop a security screening personnel examination for use in determining the qualification of individuals seeking employment as security screening personnel. The Under Secretary shall also review, and revise as necessary, any standard, rule, or regulation governing the employment of individuals as security screening personnel.

(f) EMPLOYMENT STANDARDS FOR SCREENING PERSONNEL

(1) SCREENER REQUIREMENTS- Notwithstanding any provision of law, an individual may not be deployed as a security screener unless that individual meets the following requirements:

(A) The individual shall possess a high school diploma, a general equivalency diploma, or experience that the Under Secretary has determined to be sufficient for the individual to perform the duties of the position.

(B) The individual shall possess basic aptitudes and physical abilities, including color perception, visual and aural acuity, physical coordination, and motor skills, to the following standards:

      (i)   Screeners operating screening equipment shall be able to distinguish on the screening equipment monitor the appropriate imaging standard specified by the Under Secretary.

      (ii)   Screeners operating any screening equipment shall be able to distinguish each color displayed on every type of screening equipment and explain what each color signifies.

      (iii)   Screeners shall be able to hear and respond to the spoken voice and to audible alarms generated by screening equipment in an active checkpoint environment.

      (iv)   Screeners performing physical searches or other related operations shall be able to efficiently and thoroughly manipulate and handle such baggage, containers, and other objects subject to security processing.

      (v)   Screeners who perform patdowns or hand-held metal detector searches of individuals shall have sufficient dexterity and capability to thoroughly conduct those procedures over an individual's entire body.

(C) The individual shall be able to read, speak, and write English well enough to-

      (i)   carry out written and oral instructions regarding the proper performance of screening duties;

      (ii)   read English language identification media, credentials, airline tickets, and labels on items normally encountered in the screening process;

      (iii)   provide direction to and understand and answer questions from English-speaking individuals undergoing screening; and

   (iv) write incident reports and statements and log entries into security records in the English language.

 (D) The individual shall have satisfactorily completed all initial, recurrent, and appropriate specialized training required by the security program, except as provided in paragraph (3).

 (2) VETERANS PREFERENCE- The Under Secretary shall provide a preference for the hiring of an individual as a security screener if the individual is a member or former member of the armed forces and if the individual is entitled, under statute, to retired, retirement, or retainer pay on account of service as a member of the armed forces.

 (3) EXCEPTIONS- An individual who has not completed the training required by this section may be deployed during the on-the-job portion of training to perform functions if that individual-

  (A) is closely supervised; and

  (B) does not make independent judgments as to whether individuals or property may enter a sterile area or aircraft without further inspection.

 (4) REMEDIAL TRAINING- No individual employed as a security screener may perform a screening function after that individual has failed an operational test related to that function until that individual has successfully completed the remedial training specified in the security program.

 (5) ANNUAL PROFICIENCY REVIEW- The Under Secretary shall provide that an annual evaluation of each individual assigned screening duties is conducted and documented. An individual employed as a security screener may not continue to be employed in that capacity unless the evaluation demonstrates that the individual-

  (A) continues to meet all qualifications and standards required to perform a screening function;

  (B) has a satisfactory record of performance and attention to duty based on the standards and requirements in the security program; and

  (C) demonstrates the current knowledge and skills necessary to courteously, vigilantly, and effectively perform screening functions.

 (6) OPERATIONAL TESTING- In addition to the annual proficiency review conducted under paragraph (5), the Under Secretary shall provide for the operational testing of such personnel.

(g) Training-

 (1) USE OF OTHER AGENCIES- The Under Secretary may enter into a memorandum of understanding or other arrangement with any other federal agency or department with appropriate law enforcement responsibilities, to provide personnel, resources, or other forms of assistance in the training of security screening personnel.

 (2) TRAINING PLAN- Within 60 days after the date of enactment of the Aviation and Transportation Security Act, the Under Secretary shall develop a plan for the training of security screening personnel. The plan shall require, at a minimum, that a security screener-

  (A) has completed 40 hours of classroom instruction or successfully completed a program that the Under Secretary determines will train individuals to a level of proficiency equivalent to the level that would be achieved by such classroom instruction;

  (B) has completed 60 hours of on-the-job instructions: and

  (C) has successfully completed an on-the-job training examination prescribed by the Under Secretary.

 (3) EQUIPMENT-SPECIFIC TRAINING- An individual employed as a security screener may not use any security screening device or equipment in the scope of that individual's employment unless the individual has been trained on that device or equipment and has successfully completed a test on the use of the device or equipment.

(h) TECHNOLOGICAL TRAINING-

        (1) IN GENERAL- The Under Secretary shall require training to ensure that screeners are proficient in using the most up-to-date new technology and to ensure their proficiency in recognizing new threats and weapons.

        (2) PERIODIC ASSESSMENTS- The Under Secretary shall make periodic assessments to determine if there are dual use items and inform security screening personnel of the existence of such items.

        (3) CURRENT LISTS OF DUAL USE ITEMS- Current lists of dual use items shall be part of the ongoing training for screeners.

        (4) DUAL USE DEFINED- For purposes of this subsection, the term 'dual use' item means an item that may seem harmless but that may be used as a weapon.

(i) LIMITATION ON RIGHT TO STRIKE- An individual that screens passengers or property, or both, at an airport under this section may not participate in a strike, or assert the right to strike, against the person (including a governmental entity) employing such individual to perform such screening.

(j) UNIFORMS- The Under Secretary shall require any individual who screens passengers and property pursuant to section 44901 to be attired while on duty in a uniform approved by the Under Secretary.

(b) CONFORMING AMENDMENTS- Section 44936(a)(1) of title 49, United States Code, is amended-

        (1) in subparagraph (A) by inserting as a security screener under section 44935(e) or a position' after a position'; and

        (2) in subparagraph (E) by striking clause (iv).

(c) TRANSITION- The Under Secretary of Transportation for Security shall complete the full implementation of section 44935 (e), (f), (g), and (h) of title 49, United States Code, as amended by subsection (a), as soon as is practicable. The Under Secretary may make or continue such arrangements for the training of security screeners under that section as the Under Secretary determines necessary pending full implementation of that section as so amended.

(d) SCREENER PERSONNEL- Notwithstanding any other provision of law, the Under Secretary of transportation for Security may employ, appoint, discipline, terminate, and fix the compensation, terms, and conditions of employment of Federal service for such a number of individuals as the Under Secretary determines to be necessary to carry out the screening functions of the Under Secretary under section 44901 of title 49. United States Code. The Under Secretary shall establish levels of compensation and other benefits for individuals so employed.

HOW TO TAKE A TEST

I. YOU MUST PASS AN EXAMINATION

A. *WHAT EVERY CANDIDATE SHOULD KNOW*

Examination applicants often ask us for help in preparing for the written test. What can I study in advance? What kinds of questions will be asked? How will the test be given? How will the papers be graded?

As an applicant for a civil service examination, you may be wondering about some of these things. Our purpose here is to suggest effective methods of advance study and to describe civil service examinations.

Your chances for success on this examination can be increased if you know how to prepare. Those "pre-examination jitters" can be reduced if you know what to expect. You can even experience an adventure in good citizenship if you know why civil service exams are given.

B. *WHY ARE CIVIL SERVICE EXAMINATIONS GIVEN?*

Civil service examinations are important to you in two ways. As a citizen, you want public jobs filled by employees who know how to do their work. As a job seeker, you want a fair chance to compete for that job on an equal footing with other candidates. The best-known means of accomplishing this two-fold goal is the competitive examination.

Exams are widely publicized throughout the nation. They may be administered for jobs in federal, state, city, municipal, town or village governments or agencies.

Any citizen may apply, with some limitations, such as the age or residence of applicants. Your experience and education may be reviewed to see whether you meet the requirements for the particular examination. When these requirements exist, they are reasonable and applied consistently to all applicants. Thus, a competitive examination may cause you some uneasiness now, but it is your privilege and safeguard.

C. *HOW ARE CIVIL SERVICE EXAMS DEVELOPED?*

Examinations are carefully written by trained technicians who are specialists in the field known as "psychological measurement," in consultation with recognized authorities in the field of work that the test will cover. These experts recommend the subject matter areas or skills to be tested; only those knowledges or skills important to your success on the job are included. The most reliable books and source materials available are used as references. Together, the experts and technicians judge the difficulty level of the questions.

Test technicians know how to phrase questions so that the problem is clearly stated. Their ethics do not permit "trick" or "catch" questions. Questions may have been tried out on sample groups, or subjected to statistical analysis, to determine their usefulness.

Written tests are often used in combination with performance tests, ratings of training and experience, and oral interviews. All of these measures combine to form the best-known means of finding the right person for the right job.

II. HOW TO PASS THE WRITTEN TEST

A. NATURE OF THE EXAMINATION

To prepare intelligently for civil service examinations, you should know how they differ from school examinations you have taken. In school you were assigned certain definite pages to read or subjects to cover. The examination questions were quite detailed and usually emphasized memory. Civil service exams, on the other hand, try to discover your present ability to perform the duties of a position, plus your potentiality to learn these duties. In other words, a civil service exam attempts to predict how successful you will be. Questions cover such a broad area that they cannot be as minute and detailed as school exam questions.

In the public service similar kinds of work, or positions, are grouped together in one "class." This process is known as *position-classification*. All the positions in a class are paid according to the salary range for that class. One class title covers all of these positions, and they are all tested by the same examination.

B. FOUR BASIC STEPS

1) Study the announcement

How, then, can you know what subjects to study? Our best answer is: "Learn as much as possible about the class of positions for which you've applied." The exam will test the knowledge, skills and abilities needed to do the work.

Your most valuable source of information about the position you want is the official exam announcement. This announcement lists the training and experience qualifications. Check these standards and apply only if you come reasonably close to meeting them.

The brief description of the position in the examination announcement offers some clues to the subjects which will be tested. Think about the job itself. Review the duties in your mind. Can you perform them, or are there some in which you are rusty? Fill in the blank spots in your preparation.

Many jurisdictions preview the written test in the exam announcement by including a section called "Knowledge and Abilities Required," "Scope of the Examination," or some similar heading. Here you will find out specifically what fields will be tested.

2) Review your own background

Once you learn in general what the position is all about, and what you need to know to do the work, ask yourself which subjects you already know fairly well and which need improvement. You may wonder whether to concentrate on improving your strong areas or on building some background in your fields of weakness. When the announcement has specified "some knowledge" or "considerable knowledge," or has used adjectives like "beginning principles of..." or "advanced ... methods," you can get a clue as to the number and difficulty of questions to be asked in any given field. More questions, and hence broader coverage, would be included for those subjects which are more important in the work. Now weigh your strengths and weaknesses against the job requirements and prepare accordingly.

3) Determine the level of the position

Another way to tell how intensively you should prepare is to understand the level of the job for which you are applying. Is it the entering level? In other words, is this the position in which beginners in a field of work are hired? Or is it an intermediate or advanced level? Sometimes this is indicated by such words as "Junior" or "Senior" in the class title. Other jurisdictions use Roman numerals to designate the level – Clerk I, Clerk II, for example. The word "Supervisor" sometimes appears in the title. If the level is not indicated by the title, check the description of duties. Will you be working under very close supervision, or will you have responsibility for independent decisions in this work?

4) Choose appropriate study materials

Now that you know the subjects to be examined and the relative amount of each subject to be covered, you can choose suitable study materials. For beginning level jobs, or even advanced ones, if you have a pronounced weakness in some aspect of your training, read a modern, standard textbook in that field. Be sure it is up to date and has general coverage. Such books are normally available at your library, and the librarian will be glad to help you locate one. For entry-level positions, questions of appropriate difficulty are chosen – neither highly advanced questions, nor those too simple. Such questions require careful thought but not advanced training.

If the position for which you are applying is technical or advanced, you will read more advanced, specialized material. If you are already familiar with the basic principles of your field, elementary textbooks would waste your time. Concentrate on advanced textbooks and technical periodicals. Think through the concepts and review difficult problems in your field.

These are all general sources. You can get more ideas on your own initiative, following these leads. For example, training manuals and publications of the government agency which employs workers in your field can be useful, particularly for technical and professional positions. A letter or visit to the government department involved may result in more specific study suggestions, and certainly will provide you with a more definite idea of the exact nature of the position you are seeking.

III. KINDS OF TESTS

Tests are used for purposes other than measuring knowledge and ability to perform specified duties. For some positions, it is equally important to test ability to make adjustments to new situations or to profit from training. In others, basic mental abilities not dependent on information are essential. Questions which test these things may not appear as pertinent to the duties of the position as those which test for knowledge and information. Yet they are often highly important parts of a fair examination. For very general questions, it is almost impossible to help you direct your study efforts. What we can do is to point out some of the more common of these general abilities needed in public service positions and describe some typical questions.

1) General information

Broad, general information has been found useful for predicting job success in some kinds of work. This is tested in a variety of ways, from vocabulary lists to questions about current events. Basic background in some field of work, such as sociology or economics, may be sampled in a group of questions. Often these are principles which have become familiar to most persons through exposure rather than through formal training. It is difficult to advise you how to study for these questions; being alert to the world around you is our best suggestion.

2) Verbal ability

An example of an ability needed in many positions is verbal or language ability. Verbal ability is, in brief, the ability to use and understand words. Vocabulary and grammar tests are typical measures of this ability. Reading comprehension or paragraph interpretation questions are common in many kinds of civil service tests. You are given a paragraph of written material and asked to find its central meaning.

3) Numerical ability

Number skills can be tested by the familiar arithmetic problem, by checking paired lists of numbers to see which are alike and which are different, or by interpreting charts and graphs. In the latter test, a graph may be printed in the test booklet which you are asked to use as the basis for answering questions.

4) Observation

A popular test for law-enforcement positions is the observation test. A picture is shown to you for several minutes, then taken away. Questions about the picture test your ability to observe both details and larger elements.

5) Following directions

In many positions in the public service, the employee must be able to carry out written instructions dependably and accurately. You may be given a chart with several columns, each column listing a variety of information. The questions require you to carry out directions involving the information given in the chart.

6) Skills and aptitudes

Performance tests effectively measure some manual skills and aptitudes. When the skill is one in which you are trained, such as typing or shorthand, you can practice. These tests are often very much like those given in business school or high school courses. For many of the other skills and aptitudes, however, no short-time preparation can be made. Skills and abilities natural to you or that you have developed throughout your lifetime are being tested.

Many of the general questions just described provide all the data needed to answer the questions and ask you to use your reasoning ability to find the answers. Your best preparation for these tests, as well as for tests of facts and ideas, is to be at your physical and mental best. You, no doubt, have your own methods of getting into an exam-taking mood and keeping "in shape." The next section lists some ideas on this subject.

IV. KINDS OF QUESTIONS

Only rarely is the "essay" question, which you answer in narrative form, used in civil service tests. Civil service tests are usually of the short-answer type. Full instructions for answering these questions will be given to you at the examination. But in case this is your first experience with short-answer questions and separate answer sheets, here is what you need to know:

1) Multiple-choice Questions

Most popular of the short-answer questions is the "multiple choice" or "best answer" question. It can be used, for example, to test for factual knowledge, ability to solve problems or judgment in meeting situations found at work.

A multiple-choice question is normally one of three types—
- It can begin with an incomplete statement followed by several possible endings. You are to find the one ending which *best* completes the statement, although some of the others may not be entirely wrong.
- It can also be a complete statement in the form of a question which is answered by choosing one of the statements listed.
- It can be in the form of a problem – again you select the best answer.

Here is an example of a multiple-choice question with a discussion which should give you some clues as to the method for choosing the right answer:

When an employee has a complaint about his assignment, the action which will *best* help him overcome his difficulty is to
A. discuss his difficulty with his coworkers
B. take the problem to the head of the organization
C. take the problem to the person who gave him the assignment
D. say nothing to anyone about his complaint

In answering this question, you should study each of the choices to find which is best. Consider choice "A" – Certainly an employee may discuss his complaint with fellow employees, but no change or improvement can result, and the complaint remains unresolved. Choice "B" is a poor choice since the head of the organization probably does not know what assignment you have been given, and taking your problem to him is known as "going over the head" of the supervisor. The supervisor, or person who made the assignment, is the person who can clarify it or correct any injustice. Choice "C" is, therefore, correct. To say nothing, as in choice "D," is unwise. Supervisors have and interest in knowing the problems employees are facing, and the employee is seeking a solution to his problem.

2) True/False Questions

The "true/false" or "right/wrong" form of question is sometimes used. Here a complete statement is given. Your job is to decide whether the statement is right or wrong.

SAMPLE: A roaming cell-phone call to a nearby city costs less than a non-roaming call to a distant city.

This statement is wrong, or false, since roaming calls are more expensive.

This is not a complete list of all possible question forms, although most of the others are variations of these common types. You will always get complete directions for answering questions. Be sure you understand *how* to mark your answers – ask questions until you do.

V. RECORDING YOUR ANSWERS

Computer terminals are used more and more today for many different kinds of exams.

For an examination with very few applicants, you may be told to record your answers in the test booklet itself. Separate answer sheets are much more common. If this separate answer sheet is to be scored by machine – and this is often the case – it is highly important that you mark your answers correctly in order to get credit.

An electronic scoring machine is often used in civil service offices because of the speed with which papers can be scored. Machine-scored answer sheets must be marked with a pencil, which will be given to you. This pencil has a high graphite content which responds to the electronic scoring machine. As a matter of fact, stray dots may register as answers, so do not let your pencil rest on the answer sheet while you are pondering the correct answer. Also, if your pencil lead breaks or is otherwise defective, ask for another.

Since the answer sheet will be dropped in a slot in the scoring machine, be careful not to bend the corners or get the paper crumpled.

The answer sheet normally has five vertical columns of numbers, with 30 numbers to a column. These numbers correspond to the question numbers in your test booklet. After each number, going across the page are four or five pairs of dotted lines. These short dotted lines have small letters or numbers above them. The first two pairs may also have a "T" or "F" above the letters. This indicates that the first two pairs only are to be used if the questions are of the true-false type. If the questions are multiple choice, disregard the "T" and "F" and pay attention only to the small letters or numbers.

Answer your questions in the manner of the sample that follows:

32. The largest city in the United States is
    A. Washington, D.C.
    B. New York City
    C. Chicago
    D. Detroit
    E. San Francisco

1) Choose the answer you think is best. (New York City is the largest, so "B" is correct.)
2) Find the row of dotted lines numbered the same as the question you are answering. (Find row number 32)
3) Find the pair of dotted lines corresponding to the answer. (Find the pair of lines under the mark "B.")
4) Make a solid black mark between the dotted lines.

VI. BEFORE THE TEST

Common sense will help you find procedures to follow to get ready for an examination. Too many of us, however, overlook these sensible measures. Indeed, nervousness and fatigue have been found to be the most serious reasons why applicants fail to do their best on civil service tests. Here is a list of reminders:

- Begin your preparation early – Don't wait until the last minute to go scurrying around for books and materials or to find out what the position is all about.
- Prepare continuously – An hour a night for a week is better than an all-night cram session. This has been definitely established. What is more, a night a week for a month will return better dividends than crowding your study into a shorter period of time.
- Locate the place of the exam – You have been sent a notice telling you when and where to report for the examination. If the location is in a different town or otherwise unfamiliar to you, it would be well to inquire the best route and learn something about the building.
- Relax the night before the test – Allow your mind to rest. Do not study at all that night. Plan some mild recreation or diversion; then go to bed early and get a good night's sleep.
- Get up early enough to make a leisurely trip to the place for the test – This way unforeseen events, traffic snarls, unfamiliar buildings, etc. will not upset you.
- Dress comfortably – A written test is not a fashion show. You will be known by number and not by name, so wear something comfortable.
- Leave excess paraphernalia at home – Shopping bags and odd bundles will get in your way. You need bring only the items mentioned in the official notice you received; usually everything you need is provided. Do not bring reference books to the exam. They will only confuse those last minutes and be taken away from you when in the test room.
- Arrive somewhat ahead of time – If because of transportation schedules you must get there very early, bring a newspaper or magazine to take your mind off yourself while waiting.
- Locate the examination room – When you have found the proper room, you will be directed to the seat or part of the room where you will sit. Sometimes you are given a sheet of instructions to read while you are waiting. Do not fill out any forms until you are told to do so; just read them and be prepared.
- Relax and prepare to listen to the instructions
- If you have any physical problem that may keep you from doing your best, be sure to tell the test administrator. If you are sick or in poor health, you really cannot do your best on the exam. You can come back and take the test some other time.

VII. AT THE TEST

The day of the test is here and you have the test booklet in your hand. The temptation to get going is very strong. Caution! There is more to success than knowing the right answers. You must know how to identify your papers and understand variations in the type of short-answer question used in this particular examination. Follow these suggestions for maximum results from your efforts:

1) Cooperate with the monitor

The test administrator has a duty to create a situation in which you can be as much at ease as possible. He will give instructions, tell you when to begin, check to see that you are marking your answer sheet correctly, and so on. He is not there to guard you, although he will see that your competitors do not take unfair advantage. He wants to help you do your best.

2) Listen to all instructions

Don't jump the gun! Wait until you understand all directions. In most civil service tests you get more time than you need to answer the questions. So don't be in a hurry. Read each word of instructions until you clearly understand the meaning. Study the examples, listen to all announcements and follow directions. Ask questions if you do not understand what to do.

3) Identify your papers

Civil service exams are usually identified by number only. You will be assigned a number; you must not put your name on your test papers. Be sure to copy your number correctly. Since more than one exam may be given, copy your exact examination title.

4) Plan your time

Unless you are told that a test is a "speed" or "rate of work" test, speed itself is usually not important. Time enough to answer all the questions will be provided, but this does not mean that you have all day. An overall time limit has been set. Divide the total time (in minutes) by the number of questions to determine the approximate time you have for each question.

5) Do not linger over difficult questions

If you come across a difficult question, mark it with a paper clip (useful to have along) and come back to it when you have been through the booklet. One caution if you do this – be sure to skip a number on your answer sheet as well. Check often to be sure that you have not lost your place and that you are marking in the row numbered the same as the question you are answering.

6) Read the questions

Be sure you know what the question asks! Many capable people are unsuccessful because they failed to *read* the questions correctly.

7) Answer all questions

Unless you have been instructed that a penalty will be deducted for incorrect answers, it is better to guess than to omit a question.

8) Speed tests

It is often better NOT to guess on speed tests. It has been found that on timed tests people are tempted to spend the last few seconds before time is called in marking answers at random – without even reading them – in the hope of picking up a few extra points. To discourage this practice, the instructions may warn you that your score will be "corrected" for guessing. That is, a penalty will be applied. The incorrect answers will be deducted from the correct ones, or some other penalty formula will be used.

9) Review your answers
    If you finish before time is called, go back to the questions you guessed or omitted to give them further thought. Review other answers if you have time.

10) Return your test materials
    If you are ready to leave before others have finished or time is called, take ALL your materials to the monitor and leave quietly. Never take any test material with you. The monitor can discover whose papers are not complete, and taking a test booklet may be grounds for disqualification.

VIII. EXAMINATION TECHNIQUES

1)   Read the general instructions carefully. These are usually printed on the first page of the exam booklet. As a rule, these instructions refer to the timing of the examination; the fact that you should not start work until the signal and must stop work at a signal, etc. If there are any *special* instructions, such as a choice of questions to be answered, make sure that you note this instruction carefully.

2)   When you are ready to start work on the examination, that is as soon as the signal has been given, read the instructions to each question booklet, underline any key words or phrases, such as *least, best, outline, describe* and the like. In this way you will tend to answer as requested rather than discover on reviewing your paper that you *listed without describing*, that you selected the *worst* choice rather than the *best* choice, etc.

3)   If the examination is of the objective or multiple-choice type – that is, each question will also give a series of possible answers: A, B, C or D, and you are called upon to select the best answer and write the letter next to that answer on your answer paper – it is advisable to start answering each question in turn. There may be anywhere from 50 to 100 such questions in the three or four hours allotted and you can see how much time would be taken if you read through all the questions before beginning to answer any. Furthermore, if you come across a question or group of questions which you know would be difficult to answer, it would undoubtedly affect your handling of all the other questions.

4)   If the examination is of the essay type and contains but a few questions, it is a moot point as to whether you should read all the questions before starting to answer any one. Of course, if you are given a choice – say five out of seven and the like – then it is essential to read all the questions so you can eliminate the two that are most difficult. If, however, you are asked to answer all the questions, there may be danger in trying to answer the easiest one first because you may find that you will spend too much time on it. The best technique is to answer the first question, then proceed to the second, etc.

5)   Time your answers. Before the exam begins, write down the time it started, then add the time allowed for the examination and write down the time it must be completed, then divide the time available somewhat as follows:

- If 3-1/2 hours are allowed, that would be 210 minutes. If you have 80 objective-type questions, that would be an average of 2-1/2 minutes per question. Allow yourself no more than 2 minutes per question, or a total of 160 minutes, which will permit about 50 minutes to review.
- If for the time allotment of 210 minutes there are 7 essay questions to answer, that would average about 30 minutes a question. Give yourself only 25 minutes per question so that you have about 35 minutes to review.

6) The most important instruction is to *read each question* and make sure you know what is wanted. The second most important instruction is to *time yourself properly* so that you answer every question. The third most important instruction is to *answer every question*. Guess if you have to but include something for each question. Remember that you will receive no credit for a blank and will probably receive some credit if you write something in answer to an essay question. If you guess a letter – say "B" for a multiple-choice question – you may have guessed right. If you leave a blank as an answer to a multiple-choice question, the examiners may respect your feelings but it will not add a point to your score. Some exams may penalize you for wrong answers, so in such cases *only*, you may not want to guess unless you have some basis for your answer.

7) Suggestions
   a. Objective-type questions
      1. Examine the question booklet for proper sequence of pages and questions
      2. Read all instructions carefully
      3. Skip any question which seems too difficult; return to it after all other questions have been answered
      4. Apportion your time properly; do not spend too much time on any single question or group of questions
      5. Note and underline key words – *all, most, fewest, least, best, worst, same, opposite,* etc.
      6. Pay particular attention to negatives
      7. Note unusual option, e.g., unduly long, short, complex, different or similar in content to the body of the question
      8. Observe the use of "hedging" words – *probably, may, most likely,* etc.
      9. Make sure that your answer is put next to the same number as the question
      10. Do not second-guess unless you have good reason to believe the second answer is definitely more correct
      11. Cross out original answer if you decide another answer is more accurate; do not erase until you are ready to hand your paper in
      12. Answer all questions; guess unless instructed otherwise
      13. Leave time for review

   b. Essay questions
      1. Read each question carefully
      2. Determine exactly what is wanted. Underline key words or phrases.
      3. Decide on outline or paragraph answer

4. Include many different points and elements unless asked to develop any one or two points or elements
5. Show impartiality by giving pros and cons unless directed to select one side only
6. Make and write down any assumptions you find necessary to answer the questions
7. Watch your English, grammar, punctuation and choice of words
8. Time your answers; don't crowd material

8) Answering the essay question

Most essay questions can be answered by framing the specific response around several key words or ideas. Here are a few such key words or ideas:

M's: manpower, materials, methods, money, management
P's: purpose, program, policy, plan, procedure, practice, problems, pitfalls, personnel, public relations
  a. Six basic steps in handling problems:
    1. Preliminary plan and background development
    2. Collect information, data and facts
    3. Analyze and interpret information, data and facts
    4. Analyze and develop solutions as well as make recommendations
    5. Prepare report and sell recommendations
    6. Install recommendations and follow up effectiveness

  b. Pitfalls to avoid
    1. *Taking things for granted* – A statement of the situation does not necessarily imply that each of the elements is necessarily true; for example, a complaint may be invalid and biased so that all that can be taken for granted is that a complaint has been registered
    2. *Considering only one side of a situation* – Wherever possible, indicate several alternatives and then point out the reasons you selected the best one
    3. *Failing to indicate follow up* – Whenever your answer indicates action on your part, make certain that you will take proper follow-up action to see how successful your recommendations, procedures or actions turn out to be
    4. *Taking too long in answering any single question* – Remember to time your answers properly

IX. AFTER THE TEST

Scoring procedures differ in detail among civil service jurisdictions although the general principles are the same. Whether the papers are hand-scored or graded by machine we have described, they are nearly always graded by number. That is, the person who marks the paper knows only the number – never the name – of the applicant. Not until all the papers have been graded will they be matched with names. If other tests, such as training and experience or oral interview ratings have been given, scores will be combined. Different parts of the examination usually have different weights. For example, the written test might count 60 percent of the final grade, and a rating of training and experience 40 percent. In many jurisdictions, veterans will have a certain number of points added to their grades.

After the final grade has been determined, the names are placed in grade order and an eligible list is established. There are various methods for resolving ties between those who get the same final grade – probably the most common is to place first the name of the person whose application was received first. Job offers are made from the eligible list in the order the names appear on it. You will be notified of your grade and your rank as soon as all these computations have been made. This will be done as rapidly as possible.

People who are found to meet the requirements in the announcement are called "eligibles." Their names are put on a list of eligible candidates. An eligible's chances of getting a job depend on how high he stands on this list and how fast agencies are filling jobs from the list.

When a job is to be filled from a list of eligibles, the agency asks for the names of people on the list of eligibles for that job. When the civil service commission receives this request, it sends to the agency the names of the three people highest on this list. Or, if the job to be filled has specialized requirements, the office sends the agency the names of the top three persons who meet these requirements from the general list.

The appointing officer makes a choice from among the three people whose names were sent to him. If the selected person accepts the appointment, the names of the others are put back on the list to be considered for future openings.

That is the rule in hiring from all kinds of eligible lists, whether they are for typist, carpenter, chemist, or something else. For every vacancy, the appointing officer has his choice of any one of the top three eligibles on the list. This explains why the person whose name is on top of the list sometimes does not get an appointment when some of the persons lower on the list do. If the appointing officer chooses the second or third eligible, the No. 1 eligible does not get a job at once, but stays on the list until he is appointed or the list is terminated.

X. HOW TO PASS THE INTERVIEW TEST

The examination for which you applied requires an oral interview test. You have already taken the written test and you are now being called for the interview test – the final part of the formal examination.

You may think that it is not possible to prepare for an interview test and that there are no procedures to follow during an interview. Our purpose is to point out some things you can do in advance that will help you and some good rules to follow and pitfalls to avoid while you are being interviewed.

What is an interview supposed to test?
The written examination is designed to test the technical knowledge and competence of the candidate; the oral is designed to evaluate intangible qualities, not readily measured otherwise, and to establish a list showing the relative fitness of each candidate – as measured against his competitors – for the position sought. Scoring is not on the basis of "right" and "wrong," but on a sliding scale of values ranging from "not passable" to "outstanding." As a matter of fact, it is possible to achieve a relatively low score without a single "incorrect" answer because of evident weakness in the qualities being measured.

Occasionally, an examination may consist entirely of an oral test – either an individual or a group oral. In such cases, information is sought concerning the technical knowledges and abilities of the candidate, since there has been no written examination for this purpose. More commonly, however, an oral test is used to supplement a written examination.

Who conducts interviews?

The composition of oral boards varies among different jurisdictions. In nearly all, a representative of the personnel department serves as chairman. One of the members of the board may be a representative of the department in which the candidate would work. In some cases, "outside experts" are used, and, frequently, a businessman or some other representative of the general public is asked to serve. Labor and management or other special groups may be represented. The aim is to secure the services of experts in the appropriate field.

However the board is composed, it is a good idea (and not at all improper or unethical) to ascertain in advance of the interview who the members are and what groups they represent. When you are introduced to them, you will have some idea of their backgrounds and interests, and at least you will not stutter and stammer over their names.

What should be done before the interview?

While knowledge about the board members is useful and takes some of the surprise element out of the interview, there is other preparation which is more substantive. It *is* possible to prepare for an oral interview – in several ways:

1) Keep a copy of your application and review it carefully before the interview

This may be the only document before the oral board, and the starting point of the interview. Know what education and experience you have listed there, and the sequence and dates of all of it. Sometimes the board will ask you to review the highlights of your experience for them; you should not have to hem and haw doing it.

2) Study the class specification and the examination announcement

Usually, the oral board has one or both of these to guide them. The qualities, characteristics or knowledges required by the position sought are stated in these documents. They offer valuable clues as to the nature of the oral interview. For example, if the job involves supervisory responsibilities, the announcement will usually indicate that knowledge of modern supervisory methods and the qualifications of the candidate as a supervisor will be tested. If so, you can expect such questions, frequently in the form of a hypothetical situation which you are expected to solve. NEVER go into an oral without knowledge of the duties and responsibilities of the job you seek.

3) Think through each qualification required

Try to visualize the kind of questions you would ask if you were a board member. How well could you answer them? Try especially to appraise your own knowledge and background in each area, *measured against the job sought*, and identify any areas in which you are weak. Be critical and realistic – do not flatter yourself.

4) Do some general reading in areas in which you feel you may be weak

For example, if the job involves supervision and your past experience has NOT, some general reading in supervisory methods and practices, particularly in the field of human relations, might be useful. Do NOT study agency procedures or detailed manuals. The oral board will be testing your understanding and capacity, not your memory.

5) Get a good night's sleep and watch your general health and mental attitude

You will want a clear head at the interview. Take care of a cold or any other minor ailment, and of course, no hangovers.

What should be done on the day of the interview?

Now comes the day of the interview itself. Give yourself plenty of time to get there. Plan to arrive somewhat ahead of the scheduled time, particularly if your appointment is in the fore part of the day. If a previous candidate fails to appear, the board might be ready for you a bit early. By early afternoon an oral board is almost invariably behind schedule if there are many candidates, and you may have to wait. Take along a book or magazine to read, or your application to review, but leave any extraneous material in the waiting room when you go in for your interview. In any event, relax and compose yourself.

The matter of dress is important. The board is forming impressions about you – from your experience, your manners, your attitude, and your appearance. Give your personal appearance careful attention. Dress your best, but not your flashiest. Choose conservative, appropriate clothing, and be sure it is immaculate. This is a business interview, and your appearance should indicate that you regard it as such. Besides, being well groomed and properly dressed will help boost your confidence.

Sooner or later, someone will call your name and escort you into the interview room. *This is it.* From here on you are on your own. It is too late for any more preparation. But remember, you asked for this opportunity to prove your fitness, and you are here because your request was granted.

What happens when you go in?

The usual sequence of events will be as follows: The clerk (who is often the board stenographer) will introduce you to the chairman of the oral board, who will introduce you to the other members of the board. Acknowledge the introductions before you sit down. Do not be surprised if you find a microphone facing you or a stenotypist sitting by. Oral interviews are usually recorded in the event of an appeal or other review.

Usually the chairman of the board will open the interview by reviewing the highlights of your education and work experience from your application – primarily for the benefit of the other members of the board, as well as to get the material into the record. Do not interrupt or comment unless there is an error or significant misinterpretation; if that is the case, do not hesitate. But do not quibble about insignificant matters. Also, he will usually ask you some question about your education, experience or your present job – partly to get you to start talking and to establish the interviewing "rapport." He may start the actual questioning, or turn it over to one of the other members. Frequently, each member undertakes the questioning on a particular area, one in which he is perhaps most competent, so you can expect each member to participate in the examination. Because time is limited, you may also expect some rather abrupt switches in the direction the questioning takes, so do not be upset by it. Normally, a board member will not pursue a single line of questioning unless he discovers a particular strength or weakness.

After each member has participated, the chairman will usually ask whether any member has any further questions, then will ask you if you have anything you wish to add. Unless you are expecting this question, it may floor you. Worse, it may start you off on an extended, extemporaneous speech. The board is not usually seeking more information. The question is principally to offer you a last opportunity to present further qualifications or to indicate that you have nothing to add. So, if you feel that a significant qualification or characteristic has been overlooked, it is proper to point it out in a sentence or so. Do not compliment the board on the thoroughness of their examination – they have been sketchy, and you know it. If you wish, merely say, "No thank you, I have nothing further to add." This is a point where you can "talk yourself out" of a good impression or fail to present an important bit of information. Remember, *you close the interview yourself.*

The chairman will then say, "That is all, Mr. _____, thank you." Do not be startled; the interview is over, and quicker than you think. Thank him, gather your belongings and take your leave. Save your sigh of relief for the other side of the door.

How to put your best foot forward

Throughout this entire process, you may feel that the board individually and collectively is trying to pierce your defenses, seek out your hidden weaknesses and embarrass and confuse you. Actually, this is not true. They are obliged to make an appraisal of your qualifications for the job you are seeking, and they want to see you in your best light. Remember, they must interview all candidates and a non-cooperative candidate may become a failure in spite of their best efforts to bring out his qualifications. Here are 15 suggestions that will help you:

1) Be natural – Keep your attitude confident, not cocky

If you are not confident that you can do the job, do not expect the board to be. Do not apologize for your weaknesses, try to bring out your strong points. The board is interested in a positive, not negative, presentation. Cockiness will antagonize any board member and make him wonder if you are covering up a weakness by a false show of strength.

2) Get comfortable, but don't lounge or sprawl

Sit erectly but not stiffly. A careless posture may lead the board to conclude that you are careless in other things, or at least that you are not impressed by the importance of the occasion. Either conclusion is natural, even if incorrect. Do not fuss with your clothing, a pencil or an ashtray. Your hands may occasionally be useful to emphasize a point; do not let them become a point of distraction.

3) Do not wisecrack or make small talk

This is a serious situation, and your attitude should show that you consider it as such. Further, the time of the board is limited – they do not want to waste it, and neither should you.

4) Do not exaggerate your experience or abilities

In the first place, from information in the application or other interviews and sources, the board may know more about you than you think. Secondly, you probably will not get away with it. An experienced board is rather adept at spotting such a situation, so do not take the chance.

5) If you know a board member, do not make a point of it, yet do not hide it

Certainly you are not fooling him, and probably not the other members of the board. Do not try to take advantage of your acquaintanceship – it will probably do you little good.

6) Do not dominate the interview

Let the board do that. They will give you the clues – do not assume that you have to do all the talking. Realize that the board has a number of questions to ask you, and do not try to take up all the interview time by showing off your extensive knowledge of the answer to the first one.

7) Be attentive

You only have 20 minutes or so, and you should keep your attention at its sharpest throughout. When a member is addressing a problem or question to you, give him your undivided attention. Address your reply principally to him, but do not exclude the other board members.

8) Do not interrupt

A board member may be stating a problem for you to analyze. He will ask you a question when the time comes. Let him state the problem, and wait for the question.

9) Make sure you understand the question

Do not try to answer until you are sure what the question is. If it is not clear, restate it in your own words or ask the board member to clarify it for you. However, do not haggle about minor elements.

10) Reply promptly but not hastily

A common entry on oral board rating sheets is "candidate responded readily," or "candidate hesitated in replies." Respond as promptly and quickly as you can, but do not jump to a hasty, ill-considered answer.

11) Do not be peremptory in your answers

A brief answer is proper – but do not fire your answer back. That is a losing game from your point of view. The board member can probably ask questions much faster than you can answer them.

12) Do not try to create the answer you think the board member wants

He is interested in what kind of mind you have and how it works – not in playing games. Furthermore, he can usually spot this practice and will actually grade you down on it.

13) Do not switch sides in your reply merely to agree with a board member

Frequently, a member will take a contrary position merely to draw you out and to see if you are willing and able to defend your point of view. Do not start a debate, yet do not surrender a good position. If a position is worth taking, it is worth defending.

14) Do not be afraid to admit an error in judgment if you are shown to be wrong

The board knows that you are forced to reply without any opportunity for careful consideration. Your answer may be demonstrably wrong. If so, admit it and get on with the interview.

15) Do not dwell at length on your present job

The opening question may relate to your present assignment. Answer the question but do not go into an extended discussion. You are being examined for a *new* job, not your present one. As a matter of fact, try to phrase ALL your answers in terms of the job for which you are being examined.

Basis of Rating

Probably you will forget most of these "do's" and "don'ts" when you walk into the oral interview room. Even remembering them all will not ensure you a passing grade. Perhaps you did not have the qualifications in the first place. But remembering them will help you to put your best foot forward, without treading on the toes of the board members.

Rumor and popular opinion to the contrary notwithstanding, an oral board wants you to make the best appearance possible. They know you are under pressure – but they also want to see how you respond to it as a guide to what your reaction would be under the pressures of the job you seek. They will be influenced by the degree of poise you display, the personal traits you show and the manner in which you respond.

ABOUT THIS BOOK

This book contains tests divided into Examination Sections. Go through each test, answering every question in the margin. At the end of each test look at the answer key and check your answers. On the ones you got wrong, look at the right answer choice and learn. Do not fill in the answers first. Do not memorize the questions and answers, but understand the answer and principles involved. On your test, the questions will likely be different from the samples. Questions are changed and new ones added. If you understand these past questions you should have success with any changes that arise. Tests may consist of several types of questions. We have additional books on each subject should more study be advisable or necessary for you. Finally, the more you study, the better prepared you will be. This book is intended to be the last thing you study before you walk into the examination room. Prior study of relevant texts is also recommended. NLC publishes some of these in our Fundamental Series. Knowledge and good sense are important factors in passing your exam. Good luck also helps. So now study this Passbook, absorb the material contained within and take that knowledge into the examination. Then do your best to pass that exam.

———

EXAMINATION SECTION

EXAMINATION SECTION
TEST 1

DIRECTIONS: Each question or incomplete statement is followed by several suggested
answers or completions. Select the one the BEST answers the question or
completes the statement. *PRINT THE LETTER OF THE CORRECT ANSWER
IN THE SPACE AT THE RIGHT.*

The image below is the referent for a question that will appear later in this test as an
assessment of visual memory. You may study the image for as long as you like, but will
not be allowed to refer to it later in the test.

Study the image for as long as you like, and assume that the dotted line next to the
image is the plane of a mirror. Imagine what an exact reflection would look like if it were
to appear on the opposite side of this mirror. You will be asked later to identify this
object's reflected image.

1.   The Aviation and Transportation Security Act of 2001 (ATSA) provides for each of the   1.____
following, EXCEPT

   A.   establishing a new Transportation Security Administration (TSA) within the Department of Transportation
   B.   barring non-U.S. citizens from eligibility for passenger and baggage screeners
   C.   denying passengers and screeners the right to strike as a means of collective bar-
gaining
   D.   permitting licensed commercial airline pilots to keep a locked firearm in the cockpit
as a precautionary measure

2.   Which of the following is NOT a professed purpose of the use of threat image projection   2.____
(TIP) in the X-ray screener's workplace?

   A.   Measuring how well screeners perform
   B.   Maintaining high screener alertness
   C.   Statutory compliance with the Aviation and Transportation Security Act of 2001
(ATSA)
   D.   Training screeners to identify harder-to-spot objects

3. In the X-ray image below, a screener has identified the contents of the bag as suspicious.   3.____
Assuming the bag contains a bomb, the explosive material itself is most likely contained
in the

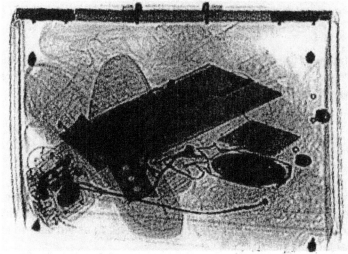

    A.   circular object on the right
    B.   pair of three-holed objects to the lower left of the image
    C.   square object at lower left, which contains a number of complex components
    D.   large rectangular mass in the center

4. In the future, explosive detection scanners will need to perform at a rate of at   4.____
least_____ bags per peak hour and_____ bags per day in order to meet goals outlined
by the Aviation and Transportation Secu-rity Act of 2001 (ATSA).

    A.   125, 800
    B.   100, 1000
    C.   225, 500
    D.   250, 1250

5. More often than not, a manual search of a piece of carry-on luggage as part of the   5.____
screener's weapon detection program will be made necessary by

    A.   a passenger being elevated to "selectee" status
    B.   suspicious passenger behavior
    C.   a suspicious x-ray image
    D.   a cluttered x-ray image

Questions 6 and 7 below test your ability to recognize an object that has been rotated in
spaceeither clockwise or counterclockwise. For each question, look at the object on the
left, and then mark A or B to indicate which of the objects to the right is correctly rotated.

6.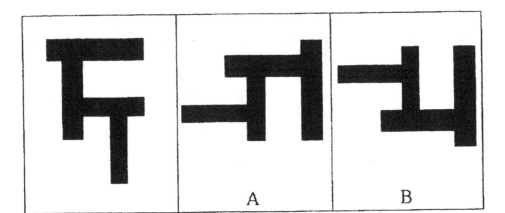

7.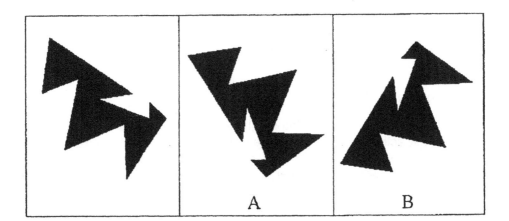

8. Which of the following items, appearing on an X-ray display, would probably be MOST suspicious to a screener?

    A. Several books that appear as dark solids
    B. A pocket calculator with two "D" cell batteries
    C. Two cameras in the same bag, only one of which appears to be loaded with film
    D. A laptop computer with an empty battery compartment

9. A passenger requests that he be allowed to take his camera through the checkpoint without passing it through the X-ray screening machine, because the camera contains film that might be damaged by X-ray examination. The passenger should be informed that

    A. normal-speed film won't be harmed by an x-ray, and no matter what kind of film is loaded into the camera, the camera itself must be x-rayed
    B. the camera can be manually searched on request if the film has already been loaded into the camera

C. high-speed film won't be harmed by an x-ray, and should be examined along with the camera itself

D. under new FAA rules, normal-speed film must be manually searched along with all cameras

10. A passenger refuses to enter a walk-through metal detector because of the possibility that the detector's electromagnetic field will interfere with the rhythm of her pacemaker. The screener should

A. conform to the requirements of the Americans with Disabilities Act (ADA) and allow the passenger to board

B. inform the passenger that her fear is unfounded and tell her there's no other way to screen her for suspicious objects

C. ask the passenger to provide medical documentation of the pacemaker's existence

D. offer to screen the passenger with a handheld metal detector

10._____

11. A passenger refuses a private screening after repeated scans with a hand-held metal detector trigger the alarm. The passenger insists that the alarm is caused by pins that were surgically implanted to repair a broken bone. The screener has no reason to disbelieve this, but nonetheless wants to per-form further screening on the passenger. In the interest of customer-oriented service, the screener's response to the passenger should begin with the words:

A. "Under federal law..."

B. "Unfortunately, we can't..."

C. "You can..."

D. "It's our policy..."

11._____

12. After several tries through the walk-through metal detector, a passen-ger in a wheelchair has repeatedly activated the alarm. The passenger himself has been examined carefully and asked to empty his pockets. The screener says she wants to take a closer look at the wheelchair itself, especially the battery case and the seat cushion. The passenger requests that this screening be done privately. Which of the following is true?

A. If the technology available makes a private check unnecessary, the screener is not required to accommodate the request.

B. Under the Americans with Disabilities Act (ADA), screeners are not permitted to give special attention to the assistive devices of the disabled.

C. Screeners are under no obligation to grant private screenings to indi-vidual, disabled or otherwise, who request them.

D. Generally, people with disabilities are not subject to the same security provisions as other passengers.

12._____

13. An explosive concealed in an item of baggage can exist as a
    I. solid
    II. liquid
    III. gas

A. I only

B. I or III

C. II or III

D. I, II or III

13._____

14. Whenever wiring appears in an X-ray image along with an electronic device, causes for suspicion include

      I.   random bundles of wire strewn about the object
     II. inconsistent quality of wiring
    III. excessive amount of wiring for the size of the object
    IV. wires that protrude outside the exterior casing of the object

   A. I and II
   B. II and III
   C. I, II and IV
   D. I, II, III and IV

14.____

15. Generally, a hand-held metal detector should be passed over the scannee's body at a distance of no more than

   A. 1 to 2 inches
   B. 3 to 4 inches
   C. 6 to 8 inches
   D. 1 to 2 feet

15.____

16. The minimum amount and configuration of a specific explosive mate-rial which would reasonably be expected to cause catastrophic damage to commercial aircraft in service is known as

   A. full throughput
   B. bulk hazard
   C. destruction threshold
   D. full level threat

16.____

17. In numerous tests over the past several decades, preboard screeners have demon-strated a fairly low probability of identifying dangerous objects, either on passengers themselves or in luggage. Conditions considered to have been important factors in these failures include

      I.   Rapid screener job turnover
     II. Inadequate attention to human factors (wages, job tasks, etc.)
    III. Inadequate technology
    IV. Poor skill sets among screeners

   A. I and II
   B. I and III
   C. I, II and IV
   D. I, II, III and IV

17.____

18. Which of the following objects, appearing in an X-ray image, has a presentation that is MOST similar to explosive material?

   A. Steel
   B. Dense cable
   C. Paper in bulk form
   D. Loosely woven fabric

18.____

19. If a passenger's body is to be scanned with a hand-held metal detector, the scan should include   19.____

    I.   armpits
    II. between the legs
    III. the head and neck
    IV. shoe soles

  A. I and IV
  B. II and III
  C. III and IV
  D. I, II, III and IV

20. This question refers to the object that appeared on page one of this test. You must work from your visual memory, and refrain from looking at the object again. Which of the following objects represents a mirror image of the previously viewed object? The plane of the mirror is supplied as a reference.   20.____

A.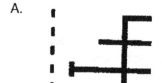

B.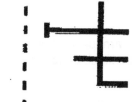

C.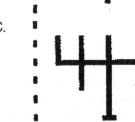

D.

21. Which of the following items is MOST likely to be the source of an alarm in a walk-through metal detector?   21.____

  A. Metal-rimmed glasses
  B. Keys
  C. Boots with steel shanks
  D. Zippers in clothing

22. A passenger's carry-on bag is discovered to contain a hypodermic syringe. The passenger is taken aside and questioned, and she produces an unmarked brown glass vial, which she says contains the insulin necessary to get her through a long flight. The screener's response to the passenger should be to   22.____

  A. immediately confiscate both the syringe and the vial
  B. allow the passenger to board the plane
  C. explain that unless the vial is packaged with a pharmaceutical or professionally printed label, neither the vial nor the syringe can be carried aboard
  D. allow the passenger to board the plane, but only if the syringe and vial are placed in the custody of a flight attendant who will supervise the injection

23. It can be reasonably expected that between_____ items per minute can be examined using an x-ray baggage scanner   23.____

    A. 5 and 10
    B. 10 and 20
    C. 20 and 30
    D. 30 and 40

24. Which of the following is NOT a procedure that should be followed in the operation of a Walk-through metal detector?   24.____

    A. If a person who causes an alarm is able to identify what must have caused the alarm, such as a belt buckle or necklace, allow the person to proceed without a rescan.
    B. To insure that scannees do not proceed to quickly through the detector, insist that they place their feet on predrawn footprints at the base of the portal within the scanning zone.
    C. Rescan to confirm that this person who has set off the alarm no longer causes an alarm after the offending item is removed from his or her possession.
    D. Never allow anyone on the outside of the cleared area the opportunity to hand something to a person who has already been cleared by the portal on the inside of the cleared area.

25. Passengers who approach a walk-through metal detector should be informed by the operator that they must place each of the following items on the conveyor belt for the x-ray machine, EXCEPT   25.____

    A. shoes/boots
    B. carried jackets
    C. purses
    D. hats

KEY (CORRECT ANSWERS)

1.	D		11.	C
2.	C		12.	A
3.	D		13.	D
4.	A		14.	D
5.	D		15.	B
6.	A		16.	D
7.	B		17.	A
8.	B		18.	C
9.	A		19.	D
10.	D		20.	C

21.	C
22.	C
23.	B
24.	A
25.	A

———

TEST 2

DIRECTIONS: Each question or incomplete statement is followed by several suggested answers or completions. Select the one the BEST answers the question or completes the statement. *PRINT THE LETTER OF THE CORRECT ANSWER IN THE SPACE AT THE RIGHT.*

The image below is the referent for a question that will appear later in this test as an assessment of visual memory. You may study the image for as long as you like, but will not be allowed to refer to it later in the test.

Study the image for as long as you like, and assume that the dotted line next to the image is the plane of a mirror. Imagine what an exact reflection would look like if it were to appear on the opposite side of this mirror. You will be asked later to identify this object's reflected image.

1. Which of the following items should be MOST suspicious to an X-ray screener?   1.____

    A.   Portable CD player with the headphones plugged in and batteries installed
    B.   Digital camera with the lens cap detached
    C.   Cell phone with a toggle switch on the front panel
    D.   An assortment of randomly strewn paperback books

2. Under current rules, a Computer Assisted Passenger Prescreening System (CAPPS)   2.____
    may use_____ as a screening factor.

    A.   race
    B.   religion
    C.   U.S. citizenship
    D.   national origin

3. The image below represents an X-ray image of a piece of luggage. The screener has identified the threat of a handgun. Which of the following presentations should also be considered suspicious?

3.____

    I.   The mass of wiring in the lower right
    II.   The dense rectangular object in the lower left
    III.   The long dark bar that extends from the top of the bag to bottom, at right
    IV.   The numerous small, dark objects scattered throughout the upper area

  A. I only
  B. I and II
  C. I, II and III
  D. I, II, III and IV

4. When a passenger is being scanned by a walk-through metal detector, it is a general rule that no other person, including the machine operator, be within a_____ -foot radius of the equipment.

4.____

  A. 3
  B. 5
  C. 10
  D. 15

5. In the X-ray screening of a bomb, the component that is often most difficult to detect is the

5.____

  A. initiator
  B. explosive
  C. power supply
  D. wiring

6. A passenger wants to take self-defense spray with her on a trip. Which of the following is/   6.____
are true?

    I. No amount of self-defense spray is allowable in carry-on luggage.
    II. While self-defense spray can't be taken on board an aircraft, there's no limit to how much may be transported in checked baggage.
    III. The amount of self-defense spray that may be transported in carry-on luggage is limited to a single 4-ounce canister.
    IV. The amount of self-defense spray that may be transported in checked luggage is limited to a single 4-ounce canister.

    A. I and II
    B. I and IV
    C. III only
    D. IV only

7. As part of his or her job, a preboard screener can expect   7.____

    I. vigorous mental and computational challenges
    II. repetitive tasks
    III. intensive monitoring
    IV. distractions that might reduce necessary vigilance

    A. I and II
    B. III only
    C. II, III and IV
    D. I, II, III and IV

8. A preboard screener is working the weekend preceding the July 4th holiday. Which of the   8.____
following items may be carried by a passenger past the preboarding security checkpoint?

    A. Butane fuel
    B. Sparklers
    C. Corkscrew
    D. Book matches

Questions 9 through 11 below test your ability to recognize an object that has been rotated in space, either clockwise or counterclockwise. For each question, look at the object on the left, and then mark A or B to indicate which of the objects to the right is correctly rotated.

9.   9._____

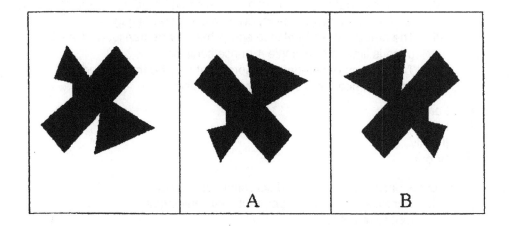

10.   10._____

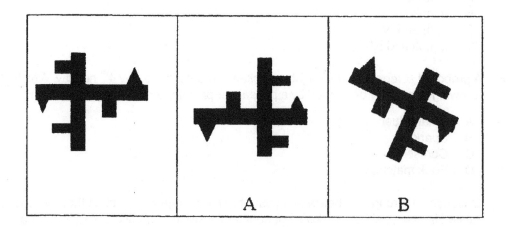

11.   11._____

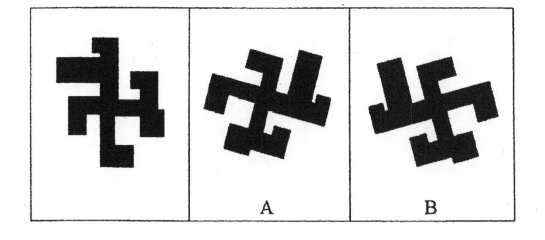

12. A middle-aged passenger who claims to have arthritis uses a walker to aid mobility. As a general rule, passengers with an assistive device   12.____

    A. should be prepared to undergo an exhaustive search of the device, including partial disassembly
    B. cannot be required to undergo special security processes if the person using the aid clears the screening system without activating it
    C. should be screened individually and privately to avoid embarrassing them
    D. should only have to undergo simple hand-held metal detection

13. Which of the following objects, appearing in an X-ray image, is MOST likely to be mistaken for explosive material?   13.____

    A. Book
    B. Shoe
    C. Small electronic device (digital camera, cell phone, etc.)
    D. Medicine

14. What is the term for the sensing of a physical or chemical property of an object that is under investigation?   14.____

    A. Bulk detection
    B. Proaction
    C. Vapor detection
    D. Trace detection

15. Which of the following is LEAST likely to be a source of electromagnetic interference for a walk-through metal detector?   15.____

    A. Fluorescent lights located directly above the operating area of the portal and within 1-2 feet of the top of the portal.
    B. Standard electrical wiring (120 volt) in a nearby wall.
    C. A metal stool or metal trash can placed close to the portal.
    D. A nearby elevator (within 10-15 feet)

16. If an explosive device is packed into a piece of luggage and screened under an X-ray machine, the power supply will usually be displayed as a(n)   16.____

    A. lighter area
    B. disorderly bundle
    C. blurry mass
    D. border without an interior mass

17. A good operator of a walk-through metal detector should expect to process between_____ people per minute, not including the investigation of alarms.   17.____

    A. 5 and 10
    B. 12 and 18
    C. 15 and 25
    D. 30 and 45

18. When analyzing an X-ray image, the most important decision a screener has to make is whether   18._____

    A. the articles contained in a bag warrant further screening of the individual who is carrying them
    B. an article represents a projected threat or a real threat
    C. a threat is explosive ornonexplosive
    D. an article is suspicious or not suspicious

19. In an x-ray image, an automatic weapon viewed from the top will most likely produce an image that is a(n)   19._____

    A. dark rectangle 4 inches or more in length
    B. distinctly gun-shaped image
    C. long tapering barrel-shaped object
    D. light square-shaped object

20. This question refers to the object that appeared on page one of this test. You must work from your visual memory, and refrain from looking at the object again. Which of the following objects represents a mirror image of the previously viewed object? The plane of the mirror is supplied as a reference.   20._____

21. In the field of aviation security, "selectees" for further screening typically include each of the following, EXCEPT passengers who   21._____

    A. are selected by computer-assisted passenger prescreening systems (CAPPS)
    B. conform to a specific racial/ethnic profile
    C. are unable to correctly answer the security questions required by the FAA's Air Carrier Standard Security Program
    D. cannot produce an approved form of identification

22. A long thin wire is concealed on the body of a passenger and taken through a walk-through metal detector at a security checkpoint. Wire such as this is MOST likely to be detected by such devices if it is

    22._____

    A. in a long straight line parallel with the side panels of the metal detector
    B. in a closed loop parallel with the side panels of the metal detector
    C. in an open loop coiled around the passenger's leg
    D. in a closed loop perpendicular to the side panels of the metal detector

23. Which of the following is NOT a provision of the Aviation and Trans-portation Security Act of 2001 (ATSA)?

    23._____

    A. The stationing of federal law enforcement officers at each airport screening check-point
    B. Enchanced use of computer profiling to screen passengers
    C. The requirement to screen at least 75% of all checked baggage on domestic and international flights
    D. The training of flight crews in anti-hijacking techniques

24. Which of the following items may be carried by a passenger past the preboarding security checkpoint?

    24._____

    A. Golf clubs
    B. 3-inch folding pocket knife
    C. Ski poles
    D. Walking cane

25. For users of hand-held metal detectors, the lower abdominal area of passengers is difficult to scan because it's a private area that is also a frequent location of metal items: belt buckles, metal buttons or snaps, and metal zippers. If an initial front body scan triggers an alarm, FIRST resorts for the screening personnel include

    25._____

    I. a more intensive search at a private location, in the presence of a supervisor who is of the same gender as the scannee
    II. asking the scannee to bend the front of his or her front waist-band forward, to ascertain that no suspicious object or weapon is hidden behind it
    III. asking the scannee to undo any belt he or she might have on, have him or her pull the belt ends away from the middle of the body, and then rescan the zipper area
    IV. a scan through a less sensitive walk-through metal detector

    A. I only
    B. I and II
    C. II and III
    D. II, III and IV

KEY (CORRECT ANSWERS)

1.	C		11.	A
2.	C		12.	B
3.	B		13.	A
4.	A		14.	A
5.	A		15.	B
6.	B		16.	A
7.	C		17.	C
8.	D		18.	D
9.	B		19.	A
10.	A		20.	B

21.	B
22.	B
23.	C
24.	D
25.	C

EXAMINATION SECTION
TEST 1

DIRECTIONS: Questions 1 through 5 are to be answered on the basis of the information, instructions, and sample question given below. Each question contains a GENERAL RULE, EXCEPTIONS, a PROBLEM, and the ACTION actually taken.

The GENERAL RULE explains what the special officer (security officer) should or should not do.

The EXCEPTIONS describe circumstances under which a special officer (security officer) should take action contrary to the GENERAL RULE.

However, an unusual emergency may justify taking an action that is not covered either by the GENERAL RULE or by the stated EXCEPTIONS.

The PROBLEM describes a situation requiring some action by the special officer (security officer).

ACTION describes what a special officer (security officer) actually did in that particular case.

Read carefully the GENERAL RULE and EXCEPTIONS, the PROBLEM, and the ACTION, and the mark A, B, C, or D in the space at the right in accordance with the following instructions:

    I.   If an action is clearly justified under the general rule, mark your answer A.
    II.   If an action is not justified under the general rule, but is justified under a stated exception, mark your answer B.
    III.   If an action is not justified either by the general rule or by a stated exception, but does seem strongly justified by an unusual emergency situation, mark your answer C.
    IV.   If an action does not seem justified for any of these reasons, mark your answer D.

SAMPLE QUESTION:

GENERAL RULE: A special officer (security officer) is not empowered to stop a person and search him for hidden weapons.
EXCEPTION: He may stop a person and search him if he has good reason to believe that he may be carrying a hidden weapon. Good reasons to believe he may be carrying a hidden weapon include (a) notification through official channels that a person may be armed, (b) a statement directly to the special officer (security officer) by the person himself that he is armed, and (c) the special officer's (security officer's) own direct observation.

PROBLEM: A special officer (security officer) on duty at a hospital clinic is notified by a woman patient at the clinic that a man sitting near her is making muttered threats that he has a gun and is going to shoot his doctor if the doctor gives him any trouble. Although the woman is upset, she seems to be telling the truth, and two other waiting patients con-

firm this. However, the special officer (security officer) approaches the man and sees no sign of a hidden weapon. The man tells the officer that he has no weapon.
ACTION: The special officer (security officer) takes the man aside into an empty office and proceeds to frisk him for a concealed weapon.

ANSWER: The answer cannot be A, because the general rule is that a special officer (security officer) is not empowered to search a person for hidden weapons. The answer cannot be B, because the notification did not come through official channels, the man did not tell the special officer (security officer) that he had a weapon, and the special officer (security officer) did not observe any weapon. However, since three people have confirmed that the man has said he has a weapon and is threatening to use it, this is pretty clearly an emergency situation that calls for action. Therefore, the answer is C.

1. GENERAL RULE: A special officer (security officer) on duty at a certain entrance is not to leave his post unguarded at any time.
   EXCEPTION: He may leave the post for a brief period if he first summons a replacement. He may also leave if it is necessary for him to take prompt emergency action to prevent injury to persons or property.
   PROBLEM: The special officer (security officer) sees a man running down a hall with a piece of iron pipe in his hand, chasing another man who is shouting for help. By going in immediate pursuit, there is a good chance that the special officer (security officer) can stop the man with the pipe.
   ACTION: The special officer (security officer) leaves his post unguarded and pursues the man.

   The CORRECT answer is:

   A. I   B. II   C. III   D. IV

2. GENERAL RULE: Special officers (security officers) assigned to a college campus are instructed not to arrest students for minor violations such as disorderly conduct; instead, the violation should be stopped and the incident should be reported to the college authorities, who will take disciplinary action.
   EXCEPTION: A special officer (security officer) may arrest a student or take other appropriate action if failure to do so is likely to result in personal injury or property damage, or disruption of school activities, or if the incident involves serious criminal behavior.
   PROBLEM: A special officer (security officer) is on duty in a college building where evening classes are being held. He is told that two students are causing a disturbance in a classroom. He arrives and finds that a fist fight is in progress and the classroom is in an uproar. The special officer (security officer) separates the two students who are fighting and takes them out of the room. Both of them seem to be intoxicated. They both have valid student ID cards.
   ACTION: The special officer (security officer) takes down their names and addresses for his report, then tells them to leave the building with a warning not to return this evening.

   The CORRECT answer is:

   A. I   B. II   C. III   D. IV

3. GENERAL RULE: A special officer (security officer) is not permitted to carry a gun while   3.____
on duty.
EXCEPTION: A special officer (security officer) who disarms a person must keep the
weapon in his possession for the brief period before he can turn it over to the proper
authorities. A special officer (security officer) who is NOT on duty may, like any other
citizen, own and carry a gun if he has a proper permit from the Police Department.
PROBLEM: A special officer (security officer) is assigned to a post where there have
been a series of violent incidents in the past few days. He feels that these incidents
could have been controlled much more easily if the people involved had seen that the
special officer (security officer) had a gun. He has a gun at home, for which he has a
valid permit.
ACTION: The special officer (security officer) brings his gun when he goes on duty. He
does not plan to use it, but just show people that he has it so that they will not start any
trouble.

The CORRECT answer is:

   A. I   B. II   C. III   D. IV

4. GENERAL RULE: No one except a licensed physician or someone acting directly under   4.____
a physician's orders may legally administer medicine to another person.
EXCEPTION: In a first aid situation, the special officer (security officer) is allowed to
help a person suffering frori a heart condition or other disease to take medicine which
the person has in his possession, provided that the person is conscious and requests
this assistance.
PROBLEM: A special officer (security officer) on duty at a public building is told that a
man has collapsed in the elevator. When the special officer (security officer) arrives at
the scene, the man is barely conscious. He cannot speak, but he points to his pocket.
The special officer (security officer) finds a pill bottle that says *one capsule in ease of
need.* The man nods.
ACTION: The special officer (security officer) puts one capsule in the man's hand and
guides the man's hand to his mouth.

The CORRECT answer is:

   A. I   B. II   C. III   D. IV

5. GENERAL RULE: In case of a fire drill or fire alarm, special officers (security officers) on   5.____
patrol in a building are to remain in their assigned areas to assist in the evacuation of
persons from the building and to make sure that no one takes advantage of the situation
by stealing property that is left unguarded.
EXCEPTION: Should there be an actual fire, special officers (security officers) will follow whatever instructions are given by the firefighters or police officers who arrive on
the scene to take charge.
PROBLEM: A special officer (security officer) is on duty patroling the fifth floor of a
building when a fire alarm sounds. The fire is in a supply closet at one end of the fifth
floor. All personnel have been evacuated from the floor. Neither police nor firemen
have yet shown up.
ACTION: The special officer (security officer) stays on the fifth floor at a safe distance
from the supply closet.

The CORRECT answer is:

   A. I   B. II   C. III   D. IV

KEY (CORRECT ANSWERS)

1. B
2. A
3. D
4. B
5. A

——————

EXAMINATION SECTION
TEST 1

DIRECTIONS: Each question or incomplete statement is followed by several suggested answers or completions. Select the one that BEST answers the question or completes the statement. *PRINT THE LETTER OF THE CORRECT ANSWER IN THE SPACE AT THE RIGHT.*

Questions 1-4.

DIRECTIONS: Questions 1 through 4 are based on the picture entitled *Contents of a Woman's Handbag*. Assume that all of the contents are shown in the picture.

<u>CONTENTS OF A WOMAN'S HANDBAG</u>

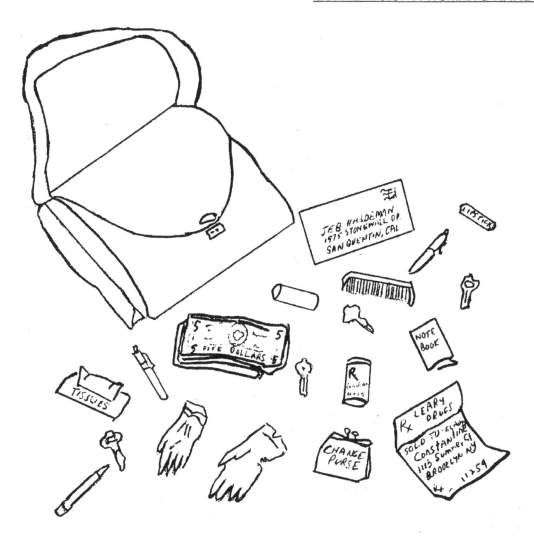

1. Where does Gladys Constantine live?   1.____

    A. Chalmers Street in Manhattan
    B. Summer Street in Manhattan
    C. Summer Street in Brooklyn
    D. Chalmers Street in Brooklyn

2. How many keys were in the handbag?   2.____

    A. 2   B. 3   C. 4   D. 5

3. How much money was in the handbag? _____ dollar(s).   3.____

    A. Exactly five   B. More than five
    C. Exactly ten   D. Less than one

4. The sales slip found in the handbag shows the purchase of which of the following?   4.____

    A. The handbag   B. Lipstick
    C. Tissues   D. Prescription medicine

Questions 5-8.

DIRECTIONS: Questions 5 through 8 are based on the floor plan below.

FLOOR PLAN

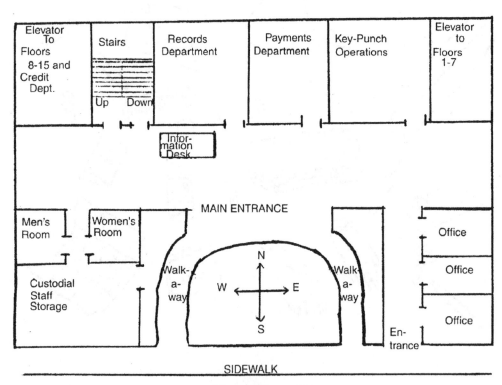

5. A special officer (security officer) on duty at the main entrance must be aware of other outside entrances to his area of the building. These unguarded entrances are usually kept locked, but they are important in case of fire or other emergency.
   Besides the main entrance, how many OTHER entrances shown on the floor plan directly face Forty-ninth Street?
   _____ other entrances.

   A. No   B. One   C. Two   D. Three

   5.____

6. A person who arrives at the main entrance and asks to be directed to the Credit Department SHOULD be told to

   A. take the elevator on the left
   B. take the elevator on the right
   C. go to a different entrance
   D. go up the stairs on the left

   6.____

7. On the east side of the entrance can be found

   A. a storage room   B. offices
   C. toilets   D. stairs

   7.____

8. The space DIRECTLY BEHIND the Information Desk in the floor plan is occupied by

   A. up and down stairs   B. key punch operations
   C. toilets   D. the records department

   8.____

Questions 9-12.

DIRECTIONS: Answer Questions 9 to 12 on the basis of the information given in the passage below.

The public often believes that the main job of a uniformed officer is to enforce laws by simply arresting people. In reality, however, many of the situations that an officer deals with do not call for the use of his arrest power. In the first place, an officer spends much of his time preventing *crimes from happening, by spotting potential violations or suspicious behavior and taking action to prevent illegal acts. In the second place, many of the situations in which officers are called on for assistance involve elements like personal arguments, husband-wife quarrels, noisy juveniles, or mentally disturbed persons. The majority of these problems do not result in arrests and convictions, and often they do not even involve illegal behavior. In the third place, even in situations where there seems to be good reason to make an arrest, an officer may have to exercise very good judgment. There are times when making an arrest too soon could touch off a riot, or could result in the detention of a minor offender while major offenders escaped, or could cut short the gathering of necessary on-the-scene evidence.*

9. The above passage IMPLIES that most citizens

   A. will start to riot if they see an arrest being made
   B. appreciate the work that law enforcement officers do
   C. do not realize that making arrests is only a small part of law enforcement
   D. never call for assistance unless they are involved in a personal argument or a husband-wife quarrel

   9.____

10. According to the passage, one way in which law enforcement officers can prevent crimes   10.____
from happening is by

    A. arresting suspicious characters
    B. letting minor offenders go free
    C. taking action on potential violations
    D. refusing to get involved in husband-wife fights

11. According to the passage, which of the following statements is NOT true of situations   11.____
involving mentally disturbed persons?

    A. It is a waste of time to call on law enforcement officers for assistance in such situations.
    B. Such situations may not involve illegal behavior
    C. Such situations often do not result in arrests.
    D. Citizens often turn to law enforcement officers for help in such situations.

12. The last sentence in the passage mentions *detention of minor offenders.*   12.____
Of the following, which BEST explains the meaning of the word *detention* as used
here?

    A. Sentencing someone
    B. Indicting someone
    C. Calling someone before a grand jury
    D. Arresting someone

Questions 13-28.

DIRECTIONS: In answering Questions 13 through 28, assume that *you* means a special
officer (security officer) on duty. Your basic responsibilities are safeguarding
people and property and maintaining order in the area to which you are
assigned. You are in uniform, and you are not armed. You keep in touch with
your supervisory station either by telephone or by a two-way radio (walkie-
talkie).

13. It is a general rule that if the security alarm goes off showing that someone has made an   13.____
unlawful entrance into a building, no officer responsible for security shall proceed to
investigate alone. Each officer must be accompanied by at least one other officer.
Of the following, which is the MOST probable reason for this rule?

    A. It is dangerous for an officer to investigate such a situation alone.
    B. The intruder might try to bribe an officer to let him go.
    C. One officer may be inexperienced and needs an experienced partner.
    D. Two officers are better than one officer in writing a report of the investigation.

14. You are on weekend duty on the main floor of a public building. The building is closed to   14.____
the public on weekends, but some employees are sometimes asked to work weekends.
You have been instructed to use cautious good judgment in opening the door for such
persons.
Of the following, which one MOST clearly shows the poorest judgment?

A. Admitting an employee who is personally known to you without asking to see any identification except the permit slip signed by the employee's supervisor
B. Refusing to admit someone whom you do not recognize but who claims left his identification at home
C. Admitting to the building only those who can give a detailed description of their weekend work duties
D. Leaving the entrance door locked for a while to make regulation security checks of other areas in the building with the result that no one can either enter or leave during these periods

15. You are on duty at a public building. An office employee tells you that she left her purse in her desk when she went out to lunch, and she has just discovered that it is gone. She has been back from lunch for half an hour and has not left her desk during this period. What should you do FIRST?   15.____

    A. Warn all security personnel to stop any suspicious-looking person who is seen with a purse
    B. Ask for a description of the purse
    C. Call the Lost and Found and ask if a purse has been turned in
    D. Obtain statements from any employees who were in the office during the lunch hour

16. You are patrolling your assigned area in a public building. You hear a sudden crash and the sound of running footsteps. You investigate and find that someone has forced open a locked entrance to the building. What is the FIRST thing you should do?   16.____

    A. Close the door and try to fix the lock so that no one else can get in
    B. Use your two-way radio to report the emergency and summon help
    C. Chase after the person whose running footsteps you heard
    D. Go immediately to your base office and make out a brief written report

17. You and another special officer (security officer) are on duty in the main waiting area at a welfare center. A caseworker calls both of you over and whispers that one of the clients, Richard Roe, may be carrying a gun. Of the following, what is the BEST action for both of you to take?   17.____

    A. You should approach the man, one on each side, and one of you should say loudly and clearly, *"Richard Roe, you are under arrest."*
    B. Both of you should ask the man to go with you to a private room, and then find out if he is carrying a gun
    C. Both of you should grab him, handcuff him, and take him to the nearest precinct station house
    D. Both of you should watch him carefully but not do anything unless he actually pulls a gun

18. You are on duty at a welfare center. You are told that a caseworker is being threatened by a man with a knife. You go immediately to the scene, and you find the caseworker lying on the floor with blood spurting from a wound in his arm. You do not know who the attacker is. What should you do FIRST?   18.____

    A. Ask the caseworker for a description of the attacker so that you can set out in pursuit and try to catch him
    B. Take down the names and addresses of any witnesses to the incident

   C. Give first aid to the caseworker, if you can, and immediately call for an ambulance

   D. Search the people standing around in the room for the knife

19. As a special officer (security officer), you have been patrolling a special section of a hospital building for a week. Smoking is not allowed in this section because the oxygen tanks in use here could easily explode. However, you have observed that some employees sneak into the linen-supply room in this section in order to smoke without anybody seeing them.
Of the following, which is the BEST way for you to deal with this situation?

   A. Whenever you catch anyone smoking, call his supervisor immediately

   B. Request the Building Superintendent to put a padlock on the door of the linen-supply room

   C. Ignore the smoking because you do not want to get a reputation for interfering in the private affairs of other employees

   D. Report the situation to your supervisor and follow his instructions

19.____

20. You are on duty at a hospital. You have been assigned to guard the main door, and you are responsible for remaining at your post until relieved. On one of the wards for which you are not responsible, there is a patient who was wounded in a street fight. This patient is under arrest for killing another man in this fight, and he is supposed to be under round-the-clock police guard. A nurse tells you that one of the police officers assigned to guard the patient has suddenly taken ill and has to periodically leave his post to go to the washroom. The nurse is worried because she thinks the patient might try to escape.
Of the following, which is the BEST action for you to take?

   A. Tell the nurse to call you whenever the police officer leaves his post so that you can keep an eye on the patient while the officer is gone

   B. Assume that the police officer probably knows his job, and that there is no reason for you to worry

   C. Alert your supervisor to the nurse's report

   D. Warn the police officer that the nurse has been talking about him

20.____

21. You are on night duty at a hospital where you are responsible for patrolling a large section of the main building. Your supervisor tells you that there have been several nighttime thefts from a supply room in your section and asks you to be especially alert for suspicious activity near this supply room.
Of the following, which is the MOST reasonable way to carry out your supervisor's direction?

   A. Check the supply room regularly at half-hour intervals

   B. Make frequent checks of the supply room at irregular intervals

   C. Station yourself by the door of the supply room and stay at this post all night

   D. Find a hidden spot from which you can watch the supply room and stay there all night

21.____

22. You are on duty at a vehicle entrance to a hospital. Parking space on the hospital grounds is strictly limited, and no one is ever allowed to park there unless they have an official parking permit. You have just stopped a driver who does not have a parking permit, but he explains that
he is a doctor and he has a patient in the hospital. What should you do?

22.____

A. Let him park since he has explained that he is a doctor
B. Ask in a friendly way, *"Can I check your identification?"*
C. Call the Information Desk to make sure there is such a patient in the hospital
D. Tell the driver politely but firmly that he will have to park somewhere else

23. You are on duty at a public building. A man was just mugged on a stairway. The mugger took the man's wallet and started to run down the stairs but tripped and fell. Now the mugger is lying unconscious at the bottom of the stairs and bleeding from the mouth. The FIRST thing you should do is to

23.____

A. search him to see if he is carrying any other stolen property
B. pick him up and carry him away from the stairs
C. try and revive him for questioning
D. put in a call for an ambulance and police assistance

24. After someone breaks into an employee's locker at a public building, you interview the employee to determine what is missing from the locker. The employee becomes hysterical and asks why you are *wasting time with all these questions* instead of going after the thief.
The MOST reasonable thing for you to do is

24.____

A. tell the employee that it is very important to have an accurate description of the missing articles
B. quietly tell the employee to calm down and stop interfering with your work
C. explain to the employee that you are only doing what you were told to do and that you don't make the rules
D. assure the employee that there are a lot of people working on the case and that someone else is probably arresting the thief right now

25. You are on duty at a public building. An employee reports that a man has just held her up and taken her money. The employee says that the man was about 25 years old, with short blond hair and a pale complexion and was wearing blue jeans.
Of the following additional facts, which one would probably be MOST valuable to officers searching the building for the suspect?

25.____

A. The man was wearing dark glasses.
B. He had on a green jacket.
C. He was about 5 feet 8 inches tall.
D. His hands and fingernails were very dirty.

26. When the fire alarm goes off, it is your job as a special officer (security officer) to see that all employees leave the building quickly by the correct exits. A fire alarm has just sounded, and you are checking the offices on one of the floors. A supervisor in one office tells you, *"This is probably just another fire drill. I've sent my office staff out, but I don't want to stop my own work."*
What should you do?

26.____

A. Insist politely but firmly that the supervisor must obey the fire rules.
B. Tell the supervisor that it is all right this time but that the rules must be followed in the future.
C. Tell the supervisor that he is under arrest.
D. Allow the supervisor to do as he sees fit since he is in charge of his own office.

27. You are on duty on the main floor of a public building. You have been informed that a   27.____
    briefcase has just been stolen from an office on the tenth floor. You see a man getting off
    the elevator with a briefcase that matches the description of the one that was stolen.
    What is the FIRST action you should take?

    A. Arrest the man and take him to the nearest public station
    B. Stop the man and say politely that you want to take a look at the briefcase
    C. Take the briefcase from the man and tell him that he cannot have it back unless he
       can prove that it is his
    D. Do not stop the man but note down his description and the exact time he got off the
       elevator

28. You are on duty at a welfare center. You have been told that two clients are arguing with   28.____
    a caseworker and making loud threats. You go to the scene, but the caseworker tells you
    that everything is now under control. The two clients, who are both mean-looking charac-
    ters, are still there but seem to be acting normally.
    What SHOULD you do?

    A. Apologize for having made a mistake and go away.
    B. Arrest the two men for having caused a disturbance.
    C. Insist on standing by until the interview is over, then escort the two men from the
       building.
    D. Leave the immediate scene but watch for any further developments.

29. You are on duty at a welfare center. A client comes up to you and says that two men just   29.____
    threatened him with a knife and made him give them his money. The client has alcohol
    on his breath and he is shabbily dressed. He points out the two men he says took the
    money.
    Of the following, which is the BEST action to take?

    A. Arrest the two men on the client's complaint.
    B. Ignore the client's complaint since he doesn't look as if he could have had any
       money.
    C. Suggest to the client that he may be imagining things.
    D. Investigate and find out what happened.

Questions 30-35.

DIRECTIONS: Answer Questions 30 through 35 on the basis of the information given in the
              passage below. Assume that all questions refer to the same state described in
              the passage.

The courts and the police consider an "offense" as any conduct that is punishable by a
fine or imprisonment. Such offenses include many kinds of acts - from behavior that is merely
annoying, like throwing a noisy party that keeps everyone awake, all the way up to violent
acts like murder. The law classifies offenses according to the penalties that are provided for
them. In one state, minor offenses are called "violations." A violation is punishable by a fine of
not more than $250 or imprisonment of not more than. 15 days, or both. The annoying behav-
ior mentioned above is an example of a violation. More serious offenses are classified as
"crimes." Crimes are classified by the kind of penalty that is provided. A "misdemeanor" is a
crime that is punishable by a fine of not more than $1,000 or by imprisonment of not more
than one year, or both. Examples of misdemeanors include stealing something with a value

of $100 or less, turning in a false alarm, or illegally possessing less than 1/8 of an ounce of a dangerous drug. A "felony" is a criminal offense punishable by imprisonment of more than one year. Murder is clearly a felony.

30. According to the above passage, any act that is punishable by imprisonment or by a fine is called a(n)

    A. offense   B. violation   C. crime   D. felony

30.____

31. According to the above passage, which of the following is classified as a crime?

    A. Offense punishable by 15 days imprisonment
    B. Minor offense
    C. Violation
    D. Misdemeanor

31.____

32. According to the above passage, if a person guilty of burglary can receive a prison sentence of 7 years or more, burglary would be classified as a

    A. violation   B. misdemeanor
    C. felony   D. violent act

32.____

33. According to the above passage, two offenses that would BOTH be classified as misdemeanors are

    A. making unreasonable noise and stealing a $90 bicycle
    B. stealing a $75 radio and possessing 1/16 of an ounce of heroin
    C. holding up a bank and possessing 1/4 of a pound of marijuana
    D. falsely reporting a fire and illegally double-parking

33.____

34. The above passage says that offenses are classified according to the penalties provided for them.
On the basis of clues in the passage, who probably decides what the maximum penalties should be for the different kinds of offenses?

    A. The State lawmakers   B. The City police
    C. The Mayor   D. Officials in Washington, B.C.

34.____

35. Of the following, which BEST describes the subject matter of the passage?

    A. How society deals with criminals
    B. How offenses are classified
    C. Three types of criminal behavior
    D. The police approach to offenders

35.____

KEY (CORRECT ANSWERS)

1. C	16. B
2. C	17. B
3. B	18. C
4. D	19. D
5. B	20. C
6. A	21. B
7. B	22. D
8. D	23. D
9. C	24. A
10. C	25. C
11. A	26. A
12. D	27. B
13. A	28. D
14. C	29. D
15. B	30. A

31. D
32. C
33. B
34. A
35. B

TEST 2

DIRECTIONS: Each question or incomplete statement is followed by several suggested answers or completions. Select the one that BEST answers the question or completes the statement. *PRINT THE LETTER OF THE CORRECT ANSWER IN THE SPACE AT THE RIGHT.*

Questions 1-5.

DIRECTIONS: Questions 1 through 5 are based on the drawing below showing a view of a waiting area in a public building.

1. A desk is shown in the drawing. Which of the following is on the desk? A(n)   1.____

    A. plant   B. telephone
    C. In-Out file   D. *Information* sign

2. On which floor is the waiting area? 2.____

    A. Basement   B. Main floor
    C. Second floor   D. Third floor

3. The door IMMEDIATELY TO THE RIGHT of the desk is a(n) 3.____

    A. door to the Personnel Office
    B. elevator door
    C. door to another corridor
    D. door to the stairs

4. Among the magazines on the tables in the waiting area are 4.____

    A. TIME and NEWSWEEK
    B. READER'S DIGEST and T.V. GUIDE
    C. NEW YORK and READER'S DIGEST
    D. TIME and T.V. GUIDE

5. One door is partly open. This is the door to 5.____

    A. the Director's office
    B. the Personnel Manager's office
    C. the stairs
    D. an unmarked office

Questions 6-9.

DIRECTIONS: Questions 6 through 9 are based on the drawing below showing the contents of a male suspect's pockets.

CONTENTS OF A MALE SUSPECT'S POCKETS

6. The suspect had a slip in his pockets showing an appointment at an out-patient clinic on   6.____

    A. February 9, 2013   B. September 2, 2013
    C. February 19, 2013   D. September 12, 2013

7. The MP3 player that was found on the suspect was made by   7.____

    A. RCA   B. GE   C. Sony   D. Zenith

8. The coins found in the suspect's pockets have a TOTAL value of   8.____

    A. 56¢   B. 77¢   C. $1.05   D. $1.26

9. All except one of the following were found in the suspect's pockets.   9.____
   Which was NOT found? A

    A. ticket stub   B. comb
    C. subway fare   D. pen

Questions 10-18

DIRECTIONS: In answering Questions 10 through 18, assume that *you* means a special officer (security officer) on duty. Your basic responsibilities are safeguarding people and property and maintaining order in the area to which you are assigned. You are in uniform, and you are not armed. You keep in touch with your supervisory station either by telephone or by a two-way radio (a walkie-talkie).

10. You are on duty at a center run by the Department of Social Services. Two teenaged   10.____
boys are on their way out of the center. As they go past you, they look at you and laugh, and one makes a remark to you in Spanish. You do not understand Spanish, but you suspect it was a nasty remark.
What SHOULD you do?

    A. Give the boys a lecture about showing respect for a uniform.
    B. Tell the boys that they had better stay away from the center from now on.
    C. Call for an interpreter and insist that the boy repeat the remark to the interpreter.
    D. Let the boys go on their way since they have done nothing requiring your intervention.

11. You are on duty at a shelter run by the Department of Social Services. You know that   11.____
many of the shelter clients have drinking problems, drug problems, or mental health problems. You get a call for assistance from a caseworker who says a fight has broken out. When you arrive on the scene, you see that about a dozen clients are engaged in a free-for-all and that two or three of them have pulled knives.
The BEST course of action is to

    A. call for additional assistance and order all bystanders away from the area
    B. jump into the center of the fighting group and try to separate the fighters
    C. pick up a heavy object and start swinging at anybody who has a knife
    D. try to find out what clients started the fight and place them under arrest

12. You have been assigned to duty at a children's shelter run by the Department of Social Services. The children range in age from 6 to 15, and many of them are at the shelter because they have no homes to go to.
Of the following, which is the BEST attitude for you to take in dealing with these youngsters?

    A. Assume that they admire and respect anyone in uniform and that they will not usually give you much trouble
    B. Assume that they fear and distrust anyone in uniform and that they are going to give you a hard time unless you act tough
    C. Expect that many of them are going to become juvenile delinquents because of their bad backgrounds and that you should be suspicious of everything they do
    D. Expect that many of them may be emotionally upset and that you should be alert for unusual behavior

12.____

13. You are on duty outside the emergency room of a hospital. You notice that an old man has been sitting on a bench outside the room for a long time. He arrived alone, and he has not spoken to anyone at all.
What SHOULD you do?

    A. Pay no attention to him since he is not bothering anyone.
    B. Tell him to leave since he does not seem to have any business there.
    C. Ask him if you can help him in any way.
    D. Do not speak to him, but keep an eye on him.

13.____

14. You are patrolling a section of a public building. An elderly woman carrying a heavy shopping bag asks you if you would watch the shopping bag for her while she keeps an appointment in the building.
What SHOULD you do?

    A. Watch the shopping bag for her since her appointment probably will not take long.
    B. Refuse her request, explaining that your duties keep you on the move.
    C. Agree to her request just to be polite, but then continue your patrol after the woman is out of sight.
    D. Find a bystander who will agree to watch the shopping bag for her.

14.____

15. You are on duty at a public building. It is nearly 6:00 P.M., and most employees have left for the day.
You see two well-dressed men carrying an office calculating machine out of the building. You SHOULD

    A. stop them and ask for an explanation
    B. follow them to see where they are going
    C. order them to put down the machine and leave the building immediately
    D. take no action since they do not look like burglars

15.____

16. You are on duty patrolling a public building. You have just tripped on the stairs and turned your ankle. The ankle hurts and is starting to swell.
What is the BEST thing to do?

16.____

A. Take a taxi to a hospital emergency room, and from there have a hospital employee call your supervisor to explain the situation.

B. First try soaking your foot in cold water for half an hour, then go off duty if you really cannot walk at all.

C. Report the situation to your supervisor, explaining that you need prompt medical attention for your ankle.

D. Find a place where you can sit until you are due to go off duty, then have a doctor look at your ankle.

17. One of your duties as a special officer (security officer) on night patrol in a public building is to check the washrooms to see that the taps are turned off and that there are no plumbing leaks.
Of the following possible reasons for this inspection, which is probably the MOST important reason?

17.____

A. If the floor gets wet, someone might slip and fall the next morning.
B. A running water tap might be a sign that there is an intruder in the building.
C. A washroom flood could leak through the ceilings and walls below and cause a lot of damage.
D. Leaks must be reported quickly so that repairs can be scheduled as soon as possible.

18. You are on duty at a public building. A department supervisor tells you that someone has left a suspicious-looking package in the hallway on his floor. You investigate, and you hear ticking in the parcel. You think it could be a bomb.
The FIRST thing you should do is to

18.____

A. rapidly question employees on this floor to get a description of the person who left the package
B. write down the description of the package and the name of the department supervisor
C. notify your security headquarters that there may be a bomb in the building and that all personnel should be evacuated
D. pick up the package carefully and remove it from the building as quickly as you can

Questions 19-22.

DIRECTIONS: Answer Questions 19 through 22 on the basis of the Fact Situation and the Report of Arrest form below. Questions 19 through 22 ask how the report form should be filled in based on the information given in the Fact Situation.

FACT SITUATION

Jesse Stein is a special officer (security officer) who is assigned to a welfare center at 435 East Smythe Street, Brooklyn. He was on duty there Thursday morning, February 1. At 10:30 A.M., a client named Jo Ann Jones, 40 years old, arrived with her ten-year-old son, Peter. Another client, Mary Alice Wiell, 45 years old, immediately began to insult Mrs. Jones. When Mrs. Jones told her to "go away," Mrs. Wiell pulled out a long knife. The special officer (security officer) intervened and requested Mrs. Wiell to drop the knife. She would not, and he had to use necessary force to disarm her. He arrested her on charges of disorderly conduct, harassment, and possession of a dangerous weapon. Mrs. Wiell lives at 118 Heally Street,

Brooklyn, Apartment 4F, and she is unemployed. The reason for her aggressive behavior is not known.

```
┌─────────────────────────────────────────────────────────────────────────────┐
│ REPORT OF ARREST                                                              │
│ ┌──────────────────────────────────────────────┬──────────────────────────┐ │
│ │ 01) _____       │ (08) _____ │ │
│ │     (Prisoner's surname)  (first)  (initial)   │       (Precinct)         │ │
│ │                                                │                          │ │
│ │ (02) _____        │ (09) _____ │ │
│ │      (Address)                                 │       (Date of arrest)   │ │
│ │                                                │       (Month, Day)       │ │
│ │ (03) _____ (04) _____ (05) _____     │ (10) _____ │ │
│ │      (Date of birth)  (Age)      (Sex)         │       (Time of arrest)   │ │
│ │ (06) _____ (07) _____     │ (11) _____ │ │
│ │      (Occupation)     (Where employed)         │       (Place of arrest)  │ │
│ └──────────────────────────────────────────────┴──────────────────────────┘ │
│ (12) _____│
│      (Specific offenses)                                                     │
│                                                                              │
│ (13) _____  (14) _____ │
│      (Arresting Officer)                      (Officer's No.)                │
└─────────────────────────────────────────────────────────────────────────────┘
```

19. What entry should be made in Blank 01?   19.____

    A. Jo Ann Jones   B. Jones, Jo Ann
    C. Mary Wiell   D. Wiell, Mary A.

20. Which of the following should be entered in Blank 04?   20.____

    A. 40   B. 40's   C. 45   D. Middle-aged

21. Which of the following should be entered in Blank 09?   21.____

    A. Wednesday, February 1, 10:30 A.M.
    B. February 1
    C. Thursday morning, February 2
    D. Morning, February 4

22. Of the following, which would be the BEST entry to make in Blank 11?   22.____

    A. Really Street Welfare Center
    B. Brooklyn
    C. 435 E. Smythe St., Brooklyn
    D. 118 Heally St., Apt. 4F

Questions 23-27.

DIRECTIONS: Answer Questions 23 through 27 on the basis of the information given in the Report of Loss or Theft that appears below.

```
┌─────────────────────────────────────────────────────────────────────┐
│ REPORT OF LOSS OR THEFT              Date: 12/4      Time: 9:15 a.m.  │
├─────────────────────────────────────────────────────────────────────┤
│ Complaint made by: Richard Aldridge          [/] Owner               │
│                                                                       │
│                    306 S. Walter St.         [x] Other - explain:     │
│                                                                       │
│                                              Head of Acctg. Dept.     │
├─────────────────────────────────────────────────────────────────────┤
│ Type of property: Computer                   Value: $550.00          │
│ Description: Dell                                                      │
│ Location: 768 N Margin Ave., Accounting Dept., 3rd Floor             │
│ Time: Overnight 12/3 - 12/4                                           │
│ Circumstances: Mr. Aldridge reports he arrived at work 8:45 A.M.,     │
│ found office door open and machine missing. Nothing else reported     │
│ missing. I investigated and found signs of forced entry: door lock    │
│ was broken.            Signature of Reporting Officer: B.L. Ramirez   │
├─────────────────────────────────────────────────────────────────────┤
│ Notify:                                                               │
│   [ ] Building & Grounds Office, 768 N. Margin Ave.                   │
│   [ ] Lost Property Office, 110 Brand Ave.                            │
│   [x] Security Office, 703 N. Wide Street                             │
└─────────────────────────────────────────────────────────────────────┘
```

23. The person who made this complaint is   23.____

    A. a secretary   B. a security officer
    C. Richard Aldridge   D. B.L. Ramirez

24. The report concerns a computer that has been   24.____

    A. lost   B. damaged   C. stolen   D. sold

25. The person who took the computer probably entered the office through   25.____

    A. a door   B. a window   C. the roof   D. the basement

26. When did the head of the Accounting Department first notice that the computer was   26.____
    missing?

    A. December 4 at 9:15 A.M.   B. December 4 at 8:45 A.M.
    C. The night of December 3   D. The night of December 4

27. The event described in the report took place at   27.____

    A. 306 South Walter Street   B. 768 North Margin Avenue
    C. 110 Brand Avenue   D. 703 North Wide Street

Questions 28-33.

DIRECTIONS: Answer Questions 28 through 33 on the basis of the instructions, the code, and the sample question given below.

Assume that a special officer (security officer) at a certain location is equipped with a two-way radio to keep him in constant touch with his security headquarters. Radio messages and replies are given in code form, as follows:

Radio Code for Situation	J	P	M	F	B
Radio Code for Action to be Taken	o	r	a	z	q
Radio Response for Action Being Taken	1	2	3	4	5

Assume that each of the above capital letters is the radio code for a particular type of situation, that the small letter below each capital letter is the radio code for the action a special officer (security officer) is directed to take, and that the number directly below each small letter is the radio response a special officer (security officer) should make to indicate what action was actually taken.

In each of the following Questions 28 through 33, the code letter for the action directed (Column 2) and the code number for the action taken (Column 3) should correspond to the capital letters in Column 1.

If only Column 2 is different from Column 1, mark your answer A.

If only Column 3 is different from Column 1, mark your answer B.

If both Column 2 and Column 3 are different from Column 1, mark your answer C.

If both Columns 2 and 3 are the same as Column 1, mark your answer D.

SAMPLE QUESTION

Column I	Column 2	Column 3
JPFMB	orzaq	12453

The code letters in Column 2 are correct, but the numbers 53 in Column 3 should be 35. Therefore, the answer is B.

	Column 1	Column 2	Column 3	
28.	PBFJM	rqzoa	25413	28._____
29.	MPFBJ	zrqao	32541	29._____
30.	JBFPM	oqzra	15432	30._____
31.	BJPMF	qaroz	51234	31._____
32.	PJFMB	rozaq	21435	32._____
33.	FJBMP	zoqra	41532	33._____

Questions 34-40.

DIRECTIONS: Questions 34 through 40 are based on the instructions given below. Study the instructions and the sample question; then answer Questions 34 through 40 on the basis of this information

INSTRUCTIONS:

In each of the following Questions 34 through 40, the 3-line name and address in Column 1 is the master-list entry, and the 3-line entry in Column 2 is the information to be checked against the master list.

If there is one line that does not match, mark your answer A.

If there are two lines that do not match, mark your answer B.

If all three lines do not match, mark your answer C.

If the lines all match exactly, mark your answer D.

SAMPLE QUESTION:

Column 1
Mark L. Field
11-09 Prince Park Blvd.
Bronx, N.Y. 11402

Column 2
Mark L. Field
11-99 Prince Park
Bronx, N.Y. 11401

The first lines in each column match exactly. The second lines do not match, since 11-09 does not match 11-99 and Blvd. does not match Way. The third lines do not match either, since 11402 does not match 11401. Therefore, there are two lines that do not match and the correct answer is B.

	Column 1	Column 2	
34.	Jerome A. Jackson 1243 14th Avenue New York, N.Y. 10023	Jerome A. Johnson 1234 14th Avenue New York, N.Y. 10023	34._____
35.	Sophie Strachtheim 33-28 Connecticut Ave. Far Rockaway, N.Y. 11697	Sophie Strachtheim 33-28 Connecticut Ave. Far Rockaway, N.Y. 11697	35._____
36.	Elisabeth N.T. Gorrell 256 Exchange St. New York, N.Y. 10013	Elizabeth N.T. Gorrell 256 Exchange St. New York, N.Y. 10013	36._____
37.	Maria J. Gonzalez 7516 E. Sheepshead Rd. Brooklyn, N.Y. 11240	Maria J. Gonzalez 7516 N. Shepshead Rd. Brooklyn, N.Y. 11240	37._____
38.	Leslie B. Brautenweiler 21 57A Seller Terr. Flushing, N.Y. 11367	Leslie B. Brautenwieler 21-75A Seiler Terr. Flushing, N.J. 11367	38._____

39. Rigoberto J. Peredes
    157 Twin Towers, #18F
    Tottenville, S.I., N.Y.

   Rigoberto J. Peredes
   157 Twin Towers, #18F
   Tottenville, S.I., N.Y.

39._____

40. Pietro F. Albino
    P.O. Box 7548
    Floral Park, N.Y. 11005

   Pietro F. Albina
   P.O. Box 7458
   Floral Park, N.Y. 11005

40._____

KEY (CORRECT ANSWERS)

1.	D	11.	A	21.	B	31.	A
2.	C	12.	D	22.	C	32.	D
3.	B	13.	C	23.	C	33.	A
4.	D	14.	B	24.	C	34.	B
5.	B	15.	A	25.	A	35.	D
6.	A	16.	C	26.	B	36.	A
7.	C	17.	C	27.	B	37.	A
8.	D	18.	C	28.	D	38.	C
9.	D	19.	D	29.	C	39.	D
10.	D	20.	C	30.	B	40.	B

EXAMINATION SECTION
TEST 1

Questions 1-4.

Questions 1 to 4 measure your ability to recognize objects, people, events, parts of maps, or crime, accident, or other scenes to which you have been exposed.

Below and on the following pages are twenty illustrations. Study them carefully. In the test, you will be shown pairs of drawings. For each pair, you will be asked which is or are from the twenty illustrations in this part.

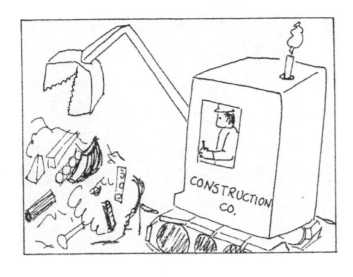

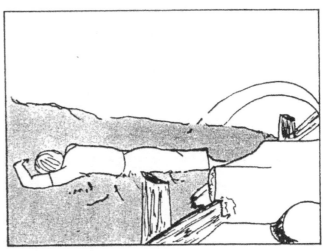

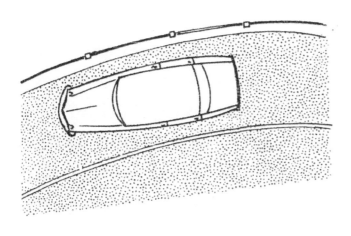

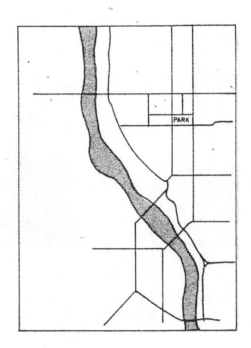

Questions 1-4.

DIRECTIONS: In Questions 1 to 4, select the choice that corresponds to the scene(s) that is(are) from the illustrations for this section. *PRINT THE LETTER OF THE CORRECT ANSWER IN THE SPACE AT THE RIGHT.*

1.

1._____

I

II.

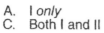

A. I *only*
C. Both I and II

B. II *only*
D. Neither I nor II

2.

2._____

I.

II.

A. I *only*
C. Both I and II

B. II *only*
D. Neither I nor II

3.

       I.

II.

A.   I *only*
C.   Both I and II

B.   II *only*
D.   Neither I nor II

4.

      I.

II.

A.   I *only*
C.   Both I and II

B.   II *only*
D.   Neither I nor II

Questions 5-6.

DIRECTIONS: Questions 5 and 6 measure your ability to notice and interpret details accurately. You will be shown a picture, below, and then asked a set of questions about the picture. You do NOT need to memorize this picture. You may look at the picture when answering the questions.

5. Details in the picture lend some support to or do NOT tend to contradict which of the fol-   5.____
lowing statements about the person who occupies the room?
       I.   The person is very careless.
      II.   The person smokes
The CORRECT answer is:

  A. I *only*   B. II *only*
  C. Both I and II   D. Neither I nor II

6.   The number on the piece of paper on the desk is *most likely* a   6.____

  A. ZIP code   B. street number
  C. social security number   D. telephone area code

Questions 7-10.

DIRECTIONS: Questions 7 to 10 measure your ability to recognize objects or people in differ-
ing views, contexts, or situations. Each question consists of three pictures; one
labeled *I,* and one labeled *II.* In each question, you are to determine whether *A
- I only, B - II only, C - Both I and II,* or *D - Neither I nor II* COULD be the Subject.
The Subject is *always* ONE person or ONE object. The Subject-picture shows
the object or person as it, he, or she appeared at the time of initial contact. Pictures I and II show objects from a different viewpoint than that of the Subject-
picture. For example, if the Subject-picture presents a front view, I and II may
present back views, side views, or a back and a side view. Also, art objects may
be displayed differently, may have a different base or frame or method of hang-
ing.

When the Subject is a person, I or II will be a picture of a different person or will be a picture of the same person after some change has taken place: The person may have made a deliberate attempt to alter his or her appearance, such as wearing (or taking off) a wig, growing (or shaving off) a beard or mustache, or dressing as a member of the opposite sex. The change may also be a natural one, such as changing a hair style, changing from work clothes to play clothes or from play clothes to work clothes, or growing older, thinner, or fatter. *None has had cosmetic surgery.*

7.　　　　　　　　　　　　　　　　　　　　　　　　　　　　　　　　　7.____

Subject　　　　　　　**I.**　　　　　　　**II.**

A. I *only*　　　　　　　　　　B. II *only*
C. Both I and II　　　　　　　D. Neither I nor II

8.　　　　　　　　　　　　　　　　　　　　　　　　　　　　　　　　　8.____

Subject　　　　　　　**I.**　　　　　　　**II.**

A. I *only*　　　　　　　　　　B. II *only*
C. Both I and II　　　　　　　D. Neither I nor II

9.

Subject

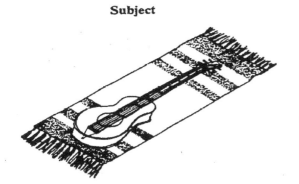

I.

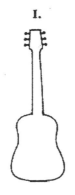

II.

9.____

A.   I *only*
C.   Both I and II

B.   II *only*
D.   Neither I nor II

10.

Subject

I.

II.

10.____

A.   I *only*
C.   Both I and II

B.   II *only*
D.   Neither I nor II

KEY (CORRECT ANSWERS)

1.	B	6.	B
2.	D	7.	D
3.	A	8.	A
4.	A	9.	D
5.	B	10.	D

READING COMPREHENSION
UNDERSTANDING AND INTERPRETING WRITTEN MATERIAL
EXAMINATION SECTION
TEST 1

DIRECTIONS: Each question or incomplete statement is followed by several suggested answers or completions. Select the one that BEST answers the question or completes the statement. *PRINT THE LETTER OF THE CORRECT ANSWER IN THE SPACE AT THE RIGHT.*

Questions 1-4.

DIRECTIONS: Questions 1 through 4 are to be answered SOLELY on the basis of the information given in the paragraph below.

Abandoned cars – with tires gone, chrome stripped away, and windows smashed – have become a common sight on the city's streets. In 2000, more than 72,000 were deposited at curbs by owners who never came back, an increase of 15,000 from the year before and more than 30 times the number abandoned a decade ago. In January 2001, the city Environmental Protection Administrator asked the State Legislature to pass a law requiring a buyer of a new automobile to deposit $100 and an owner of an automobile at the time the law takes effect to deposit $50 with the State Department of Motor Vehicles. In return, they would be given a certificate of deposit which would be passed on to each succeeding owner. The final owner would get the deposit money back if he could present proof that he has disposed of his car *in an environmentally acceptable manner.* The Legislature has given no indication that it plans to rush ahead on the matter.

1. The number of cars abandoned in the city streets in 1990 was MOST NEARLY   1.____

    A. 2,500   B. 12,000   C. 27,500   D. 57,000

2. The proposed law would require a person who owned a car bought before the law was passed to deposit   2.____

    A. $100 with the State Department of Motor Vehicles
    B. $50 with the Environmental Protection Administration
    C. $100 with the State Legislature
    D. $50 with the State Department of Motor Vehicles

3. The proposed law would require the State to return the deposit money ONLY when the   3.____

    A. original owner of the car shows proof that he sold it
    B. last owner of the car shows proof that he got rid of the car in a satisfactory way
    C. owner of a car shows proof that he has transferred the certificate of deposit to the next owner
    D. last owner of a car returns the certificate of deposit

4. The MAIN idea or theme of the above article is that

    4.____

- A. a proposed new law would make it necessary for car owners in the State to pay additional taxes
- B. the State Legislature is against a proposed law to require deposits from automobile owners to prevent them from abandoning their cars
- C. the city is trying to find a solution for the increasing number of cars abandoned on its streets
- D. to pay for the removal of abandoned cars the city's Environmental Protection Administrator has asked the State to fine automobile owners who abandon their vehicles

Questions 5-7.

DIRECTIONS: Questions 5 through 7 are to be answered SOLELY on the basis of the information given in the paragraph below.

    The regulations applying to parking meters provide that the driver is required to deposit the appropriate coin immediately upon parking and it is illegal for him to return at a later period to extend the parking time. If there is unused time on a parking meter, another car may be parked for a period not to exceed the unused time without the deposit of a coin. Operators of commercial vehicles are not required to deposit coins while loading or unloading expeditiously. By definition, a vehicle is considered parked even though there is a driver at the wheel and the meter must be used by the driver of such car.

5. According to the above paragraph, the regulations applying to parking meters do NOT

    5.____

- A. allow the driver of a parked vehicle to stay in his car
- B. consider any loading or unloading of a vehicle as parking
- C. make any distinction between an unoccupied car and one with the driver at the wheel
- D. permit a driver who has parked a car at a meter with unused parking time to put a coin in the meter

6. According to the above paragraph, it is a violation of the parking meter regulations to

    6.____

- A. load and unload slowly
- B. park commercial vehicles except for loading and unloading
- C. put a second coin in the meter in order to park longer
- D. use a parking space at any time without depositing a coin

7. The above paragraph CLEARLY indicates

    7.____

- A. the number of minutes a vehicle may be parked
- B. the value of the coin that is to be put in the meter
- C. what is meant by a commercial vehicle
- D. when a car may be parked free

Questions 8-13.

DIRECTIONS: Questions 8 through 13 are to be answered on the basis of the information
given in the paragraph below.

There are many types of reports. One of these is the field report, which requests information specified and grouped under columns or headings. A detailed, printed form is often used
in submitting field reports. However, these printed, standardized forms provide a limited
amount of space. The field man is required to make the decision as to how much of the information he has should go directly into the report and how much should be left for clarification if
and when he is called in to explain a reported finding. In many instances, the addition of a
short explanation of the finding might relieve the reader of the report of the necessity to seek
an explanation. Therefore, the basic factual information asked for by the printed report form
should often be clarified by some simple explanatory statement. If this is done, the reported
finding becomes meaningful to the reader of the report who is far from the scene of the subject matter dealt with in the report. The significance of that which is reported finds its expres-
sion in the adoption of certain policies, improvements, or additions essential to furthering the
effectiveness of the program.

8.   According to the above paragraph, the field report asks for   8.____

    A.   a detailed statement of the facts
    B.   field information which comes under the heading of technical data
    C.   replies to well-planned questions
    D.   specific information in different columns

9.   According to the above paragraph, the usual printed field report form   9.____

    A.   does not have much room for writing
    B.   is carefully laid out
    C.   is necessary for the collection of facts
    D.   usually has from three to four columns

10.   According to the above paragraph, the man in the field MUST decide if   10.____

    A.   a report is needed at all
    B.   he should be called in to explain a reported finding
    C.   he should put all the information he has into the report
    D.   the reader of the report is justified in seeking an explanation

11.   According to the above paragraph, the man in the field may be required to   11.____

    A.   be acquainted with the person or persons who will read his report
    B.   explain the information he reports
    C.   give advice on specific problems
    D.   keep records of the amount of work he completes

12.   According to the above paragraph, the value of an explanatory statement added to the   12.____
factual information reported in the printed forms is that it

    A.   allows the person making the report to express himself briefly
    B.   forces the person making the report to think logically
    C.   helps the report reader understand the facts reported
    D.   makes it possible to turn in the report later

13. According to the above paragraph, the importance of the information given by the field man in his report is shown by the   13.____

    A. adoption of policies and improvements
    B. effectiveness of the field staff
    C. fact that such a report is required
    D. necessary cost studies to back up the facts

Questions 14-15.

DIRECTIONS: Questions 14 and 15 are to be answered on the basis of the information contained in the following paragraph.

The driver of the collection crew shall at all times remain in or on a department vehicle in which there is revenue. In the event such driver must leave the vehicle, he shall designate one of the other members of the crew to remain in or on the vehicle. The member of the crew so designated by the driver shall remain in or on the vehicle until relieved by the driver or another member of the crew. The vehicle may be left unattended only when there is no revenue contained therein provided, however, that in that event the vehicle shall be locked. The loss of any vehicle or any of its contents, including revenue, resulting from any deviation from this rule, shall be the responsibility of the member or members of crew who shall be guilty of such deviation.

14. The vehicle of a collection crew may be left with no one in it only if   14.____

    A. it is locked
    B. there is a crew member nearby
    C. there is no money in it
    D. there is only one member in the crew

15. If money is stolen from an unattended vehicle of a collection crew, the employee held responsible is the   15.____

    A. driver
    B. one who left the vehicle unattended
    C. one who left the vehicle unlocked
    D. one who relieved the driver

Questions 16-18.

DIRECTIONS: Questions 16 through 18 are to be answered SOLELY on the basis of the information given in the paragraph below.

Safety belts provide protection for the passengers of a vehicle by preventing them from crashing around inside if the vehicle is involved in a collision. They operate on the principle similar to that used in the packaging of fragile items. You become a part of the vehicle package, and you are kept from being tossed about inside if the vehicle is suddenly decelerated. Many injury-causing collisions at low speeds, for example at city intersections, could have been injury-free if the occupants had fastened their safety belts. There is a double advantage to the driver in that it not only protects him from harm, but prevents him from being yanked away from the wheel, thereby permitting him to maintain control of the car.

16. The principle on which seat belts work is that

    A. a car and its driver and passengers are fragile
    B. a person fastened to the car will not be thrown around when the car slows down suddenly
    C. the driver and passengers of a car that is suddenly decelerated will be thrown forward
    D. the driver and passengers of an automobile should be packaged the way fragile items are packaged

16.____

17. We can assume from the above passage that safety belts should be worn at all times because you can never tell when

    A. a car will be forced to turn off onto another road
    B. it will be necessary to shift into low gear to go up a hill
    C. you will have to speed up to pass another car
    D. a car may have to come to a sudden stop

17.____

18. Besides preventing injury, an ADDITIONAL benefit from the use of safety belts is that

    A. collisions are fewer
    B. damage to the car is kept down
    C. the car can be kept under control
    D. the number of accidents at city intersections is reduced

18.____

Questions 19-24.

DIRECTIONS: Questions 19 through 24 are to be answered on the basis of the following reading passage covering Procedures For Patrol.

PROCEDURES FOR PATROL

The primary function of all Parking Enforcement Agents assigned to patrol duty shall be to patrol assigned areas and issue summonses to violators of various sections of the City Traffic Regulations, which sections govern the parking or operation of vehicles. Parking Enforcement Agents occasionally may be called upon to distribute educational pamphlets and perform other work, at the discretion of the Bureau Chief.

Each Agent on patrol duty will be assigned a certain area (or areas) to be patrolled. These areas will be assigned during the daily roll call. Walking Cards will describe the street locations of the patrol and the manner in which the patrol is to be walked.

A Traffic Department vehicle will be provided for daily patrol assignments when necessary.

Each Agent shall accomplish an assigned field patrol in the following manner:

    a. Start each patrol at the location specified on the daily patrol sheet, and proceed as per walking instructions.
    b. Approach each metered space being utilized (each metered space in which a vehicle is parked). If the meter shows the expired flag, the member of the force shall prepare and affix a summons to the vehicle parked at meter.

c. Any vehicle in violation of any regulation governing the parking, standing, stopping, or movement of vehicles will be issued a summons.

d. No summons will be issued to a vehicle displaying an authorized vehicle identification plate of the Police Department unless the vehicle is parked in violation of the No Standing, No Stopping, Hydrant, Bus Stop, or Double Parking Regulations. Identification plates for Police Department automobiles are made of plastic and are of rectangular shape, 10 3/4" long, 3 3/4" high, black letters and numerals on a white background. The words *POLICE DEPT.* are printed on the face with the identification number. Identification plates for private automobiles are the same size and shape as those used on Police Department automobiles.

An Agent on patrol, when observing a person *feeding* a street meter (placing an additional coin in a meter so as to leave the vehicle parked for an additional period) shall prepare and affix a summons to the vehicle.

An Agent on patrol shall note on a computer card each missing or defective, out of order, or otherwise damaged meter.

19. Of the following, the work which the Parking Enforcement Agent performs MOST often is   19._____

    A. issuing summonses for parking violations
    B. distributing educational pamphlets
    C. assisting the Bureau Chief
    D. driving a city vehicle

20. The area to be covered by a Parking Enforcement Agent on patrol is   20._____

    A. determined by the Police Department
    B. regulated by the city Traffic Regulations
    C. marked off with red flags
    D. described on Walking Cards

21. A Parking Enforcement Agent reports a broken meter by   21._____

    A. issuing a summons
    B. making a mark on a computer card
    C. raising the flag on the broken meter
    D. attending a daily roll call

22. With respect to the use of an automobile for patrol duty,   22._____

    A. Parking Enforcement Agents must supply their own cars for patrol
    B. automobiles for patrol will be supplied by the Police Department
    C. Parking Enforcement Agents are permitted to park in a bus stop
    D. department vehicles will be provided when required for patrol

23. Parking Enforcement Agents sometimes issue summonses to drivers for *feeding* a street meter in violation of parking regulations.   23._____
Which one of the following situations describes such a violation?
A driver

    A. has moved from one metered space to another
    B. has parked next to a Police Department No Standing sign
    C. is parked by a meter which shows 30 minutes time still remaining
    D. has used a coin to reset the meter after his first time period expired

24. Vehicles displaying an authorized vehicle identification plate of the Police Department
are allowed to park at expired meters.
Which one of the following statements describes the proper size of identification plates
for private automobiles used for police work?
They

    24.____

   A. are 10 3/4" long and 3 3/4" high
   B. have white letters and numerals on a black background
   C. are 3 3/4" long and 10 3/4" high
   D. have black letters and numerals on a white background

Questions 25-30.

DIRECTIONS: Questions 25 through 30 are to be answered on the basis of the following
reading passage covering the Operation of Department Motor Vehicles.

OPERATION OF DEPARTMENT MOTOR VEHICLES

When operating a Traffic Department motor vehicle, a member of the force must show
every courtesy to other drivers, obey all traffic signs and traffic regulations, obey all other law-
ful authority, and handle the vehicle in a manner which will foster safety practices in others
and create a favorable impression of the Bureau, the Department, and the City. The operator
and passengers MUST use the safety belts.

Driving Rules

   a. DO NOT operate a mechanically defective vehicle.
     DO NOT race engine on starting.
     DO NOT tamper with mechanical equipment.
     DO NOT run engine if there is an indication of low engine oil pressure, overheating,
     or no transmission oil.

   b. When parking on highway, all safety precautions must be observed.

   c. When parking in a garage or parking field, observe a maximum speed of 5 miles
     per hour. Place shift lever in park or neutral position, effectively apply hand brake,
     then shut off all ignition and light switches to prevent excess battery drain, and
     close all windows.

Reporting Defects

   a. Report all observed defects on Drivers' Vehicle Defect Card and on Monthly Vehi-
     cle Report Form 49 in sufficient detail so a mechanic can easily locate the source
     of trouble.
   b. Enter vehicle road service calls and actual time of occurrence on Monthly Vehicle
     Report.

Reporting Accidents

Promptly report all facts of each accident as follows: For serious accidents, including those involving personal injury, call your supervisor as soon as possible. Give all the appropriate information about the accident to your supervisor. Record vehicle registration information, including the name of the registered owner, the state, year, and serial number, and the classification marking on the license plates. Also record the operator's license number and other identifying information, and, if it applies, the injured person's age and sex. Give a full description of how the accident happened, and what happened following the accident, including the vehicles in collision, witnesses, police badge number, hospital, condition of road surface, time of day, weather conditions, location (near, far, center of intersection), and damage.

Repairs to Automobiles

When a Department motor vehicle requires repairs that cannot be made by the operator, or requires replacement of parts or accessories (including tires and tubes), or requires towing, the operator shall notify the District Commander.

When a Departmental motor vehicle is placed out of service for repairs, the Regional Commander shall assign another vehicle, if available.

Daily Operator's Report

The operator of a Department automobile shall keep a daily maintenance record of the vehicle, and note any unusual occurrences, on the Daily Operator's Report.

25. Parking Enforcement Agents who are assigned to operate Department motor vehicles on patrol are expected to   25.____

    A. disregard the posted speed limits to save time
    B. remove their seat belts on short trips
    C. show courtesy to other drivers on the road
    D. take the right of way at all intersections

26. The driver of a Department motor vehicle should   26.____

    A. leave the windows open when parking the vehicle in a garage
    B. drive the vehicle at approximately 10 miles per hour in a parking field
    C. be alert for indication of low engine oil pressure and overheated engine
    D. start a cold vehicle by racing the engine for 5 minutes

27. The reason that all defects on a Department vehicle that have been observed by its driver should be noted on a Monthly Vehicle Report Form 49 is: 27.____

    A. This action will foster better safety practices among other Agents
    B. The source of the defect may be located easily by a trained mechanic
    C. All the facts of an accident will be reported promptly
    D. The District Commander will not have to make road calls

28. If the driver of a Department vehicle is involved in an accident, an Accident Report should be made out. This Report should include a full description of how the accident happened.
Which of the following statements would PROPERLY belong in an Accident Report?

    A. The accident occurred at the intersection of Broadway and 42nd Street.
    B. The operator of the Department motor vehicle replaced the windshield wiper.
    C. The vehicle was checked for gas and water before the patrol began.
    D. A bus passed two parked vehicles.

28.____

29. When a Department vehicle is disabled, whom should the operator notify? The

    A. Traffic Department garage
    B. Assistant Bureau Chief
    C. Police Department
    D. District Commander

29.____

30. The PROPER way for an operator of a Department vehicle to report unusual occurrences with respect to the operation of the vehicle is to

    A. follow the same procedures as for reporting a defect
    B. request the Regional Commander to assign another vehicle
    C. phone the Bureau Chief as soon as possible
    D. make a note of the circumstances on the Daily Operator's Report

30.____

KEY (CORRECT ANSWERS)

1.	A	16.	B
2.	D	17.	D
3.	B	18.	C
4.	C	19.	A
5.	C	20.	D
6.	C	21.	B
7.	D	22.	D
8.	D	23.	D
9.	A	24.	A
10.	C	25.	C
11.	B	26.	C
12.	C	27.	B
13.	A	28.	A
14.	C	29.	D
15.	B	30.	D

TEST 2

DIRECTIONS: Each question or incomplete statement is followed by several suggested answers or completions. Select the one that BEST answers the question or completes the statement. *PRINT THE LETTER OF THE CORRECT ANSWER IN THE SPACE AT THE RIGHT.*

Questions 1-4.

DIRECTIONS: Questions 1 through 4 are to be answered SOLELY on the basis of the information contained in the following passage.

Of those arrested in the city in 2003 for felonies or misdemeanors, only 32% were found guilty of any charge. Fifty-six percent of such arrestees were acquitted or had their cases dismissed. 11% failed to appear for trial, and 1% received other dispositions. Of those found guilty, only 7.4% received any sentences of over one year in jail. Only 50% of those found guilty were sentenced to any further time in jail. When considered with the low probability of arrests for most crimes, these figures make it clear that the crime control system in the city poses little threat to the average criminal. Delay compounds the problem. The average case took four appearances for disposition after arraignment. Twenty percent of all cases took eight or more appearances to reach a disposition. Forty-four percent of all cases took more than one year to disposition.

1. According to the above passage, crime statistics for 2003 indicate that   1.____

    A. there is a low probability of arrests for all crimes in the city
    B. the average criminal has much to fear from the law in the city
    C. over 10% of arrestees in the city charged with felonies or misdemeanors did not show up for trial
    D. criminals in the city are less likely to be caught than criminals in the rest of the country

2. The percentage of those arrested in 2003 who received sentences of over one year in jail amounted to MOST NEARLY   2.____

    A. .237   B. 2.4   C. 23.7   D. 24.0

3. According to the above passage, the percentage of arrestees in 2003 who were found guilty was   3.____

    A. 20% of those arrested for misdemeanors
    B. 11% of those arrested for felonies
    C. 50% of those sentenced to further time in jail
    D. 32% of those arrested for felonies or misdemeanors

4. According to the above paragraph, the number of appearances after arraignment and before disposition amounted to   4.____

    A. an average of four
    B. eight or more in 44% of the cases
    C. over four for cases which took more than a year
    D. between four and eight for most cases

Questions 5-6.

DIRECTIONS: Questions 5 and 6 are to be answered on the basis of the following paragraph.

A person who, with the intent to deprive or defraud another of the use and benefit of property or to appropriate the same to the use of the taker, or of any other person other than the true owner, wrongfully takes, obtains or withholds, by any means whatever, from the possession of the true owner or of any other person any money, personal property, thing in action, evidence of debt or contract, or article of value of any kind, steals such property and is guilty of larceny.

5. This definition from the Penal Law has NO application to the act of   5._____

    A.   fraudulent conversion by a vendor of city sales tax money collected from purchas-
         ers
    B.   refusing to give proper change after a purchaser has paid for an article in cash
    C.   receiving property stolen from the rightful owner
    D.   embezzling money from the rightful owner

6. According to the above paragraph, an auto mechanic who claimed to have a lien on an   6._____
    automobile for completed repairs and refused to surrender possession until the bill was
    paid

    A.   *cannot* be charged with larceny because his repairs increased the value of the car
    B.   *can* be charged with larceny because such actual possession can be construed to
         include intent to deprive the owner of use of the car
    C.   *cannot* be charged with larceny because the withholding is temporary and such
         possession is not an evidence of debt
    D.   *cannot* be charged with larceny because intent to defraud is lacking

Questions 7-12.

DIRECTIONS: Questions 7 through 12 are to be answered on the basis of the information
              given in the passage below. Assume that all questions refer to the same state
              described in the passage.

The courts and the police consider an *offense* as any conduct that is punishable by a fine or imprisonment. Such offenses include many kinds of acts—from behavior that is merely annoying, like throwing a noisy party that keeps everyone awake, all the way up to violent acts like murder. The law classifies offenses according to the penalties that are provided for them. In one state, minor offenses are called *violations*. A violation is punishable by a fine of not more than $250 or imprisonment of not more than 15 days, or both. The annoying behavior mentioned above is an example of a violation. More serious offenses are classified as *crimes*. Crimes are classified by the kind of penalty that is provided. A *misdemeanor* is a crime that is punishable by a fine of not more than $1,000 or by imprisonment of not more than 1 year, or both. Examples of misdemeanors include stealing something with a value of $100 or less, turning in a false alarm, or illegally possessing less than 1/8 of an ounce of a dangerous drug. A *felony* is a criminal offense punishable by imprisonment of more than 1 year. Murder is clearly a felony.

7. According to the above passage, any act that is punishable by imprisonment or by a fine   7.____
is called a(n)

    A. offense   B. violation   C. crime   D. felony

8. According to the above passage, which of the following is classified as a crime?   8.____

    A. Offense punishable by 15 days imprisonment
    B. Minor offense
    C. Violation
    D. Misdemeanor

9. According to the above passage, if a person guilty of burglary can receive a prison sen-   9.____
tence of 7 years or more, burglary would be classified as a

    A. violation   B. misdemeanor
    C. felony   D. violent act

10. According to the above passage, two offenses that would BOTH be classified as misde-   10.____
meanors are

    A. making unreasonable noise, and stealing a $90 bicycle
    B. stealing a $75 radio, and possessing 1/16 of an ounce of heroin
    C. holding up a bank, and possessing 1/4 of a pound of marijuana
    D. falsely reporting a fire, and illegally double-parking

11. The above passage says that offenses are classified according to the penalties provided   11.____
for them.
On the basis of clues in the passage, who probably decides what the maximum penalties should be for the different kinds of offenses?

    A. The State lawmakers   B. The City police
    C. The Mayor   D. Officials in Washington, D.C.

12. Of the following, which BEST describes the subject matter of the passage?   12.____

    A. How society deals with criminals
    B. How offenses are classified
    C. Three types of criminal behavior
    D. The police approach to offenders

Questions 13-20.

DIRECTIONS: Questions 13 through 20 are to be answered SOLELY on the basis of the following passage.

Auto theft is prevalent and costly. In 2005, 486,000 autos valued at over $500 million
were stolen. About 28 percent of the inhabitants of Federal prisons are there as a result of
conviction of interstate auto theft under the Dyer Act. In California alone, auto thefts cost the
criminal justice system approximately $60 million yearly.

The great majority of auto theft is for temporary use rather than resale, as evidenced by
the fact that 88 percent of autos stolen in 2005 were recovered. In Los Angeles, 64 percent of
stolen autos that were recovered were found within two days, and about 80 percent within a

week. Chicago reports that 71 percent of the recovered autos were found within four miles of the point of theft. The FBI estimates that 8 percent of stolen cars are taken for the purpose of stripping them for parts, 12 percent for resale, and 5 percent for use in another crime. Auto thefts are primarily juvenile acts. Although only 21 percent of all arrests for nontraffic offenses in 2005 were of individuals under 18 years of age, 63 percent of auto theft arrests were of persons under 18. Auto theft represents the start of many criminal careers; in an FBI sample of juvenile auto theft offenders, 41 percent had no prior arrest record.

13. In the above passage, the discussion of the reasons for auto theft does NOT include the percent of   13.____

    A.   autos stolen by prior offenders
    B.   recovered stolen autos found close to the point of theft
    C.   stolen autos recovered within a week
    D.   stolen autos which were recovered

14. Assuming the figures in the above passage remain constant, you may logically estimate the cost of auto thefts to the California criminal justice system over a five-year period beginning in 2005 to have been about _____ million.   14.____

    A. $200   B. $300   C. $440   D. $500

15. According to the above passage, the percent of stolen autos in Los Angeles which were not recovered within a week was _____ percent.   15.____

    A. 12   B. 20   C. 29   D. 36

16. According to the above passage, MOST auto thefts are committed by   16.____

    A.   former inmates of Federal prisons   B.   juveniles
    C.   persons with a prior arrest record   D.   residents of large cities

17. According to the above passage, MOST autos are stolen for   17.____

    A.   resale   B.   stripping of parts
    C.   temporary use   D.   use in another crime

18. According to the above passage, the percent of persons arrested for auto theft who were under 18   18.____

    A.   equals nearly the same percent of stolen autos which were recovered
    B.   equals nearly two-thirds of the total number of persons arrested for nontraffic offenses
    C.   is the same as the percent of persons arrested for nontraffic offenses who were under 18
    D.   is three times the percent of persons arrested for nontraffic offenses who were under 18

19. An APPROPRIATE title for the above passage is   19.____

    A.   HOW CRIMINAL CAREERS BEGIN
    B.   RECOVERY OF STOLEN CARS
    C.   SOME STATISTICS ON AUTO THEFT
    D.   THE COSTS OF AUTO THEFT

20. Based on the above passage, the number of cars taken for use in another crime in 2005 was   20.____

    A. 24,300   B. 38,880   C. 48,600   D. 58,320

Questions 21-22.

DIRECTIONS: Questions 21 and 22 are to be answered SOLELY on the basis of the following paragraph.

If the second or third felony is such that, upon a first conviction, the offender would be punishable by imprisonment for any term less than his natural life, then such person must be sentenced to imprisonment for an indeterminate term, the minimum of which shall be not less than one-half of the longest term prescribed upon a first conviction, and the maximum of which shall be not longer than twice such longest term, provided, however, that the minimum sentence imposed hereunder upon such second or third felony offender shall in no case be less than five years; except that where the maximum punishment for a second or third felony offender hereunder is five years or less, the minimum sentence must be not less than two years.

21. According to the above paragraph, a person who has a second felony conviction shall receive as a sentence for that second felony an indeterminate term   21.____

    A. not less than twice the minimum term prescribed upon a first conviction as a maximum
    B. not less than one-half the maximum term of his first conviction as a minimum
    C. not more than twice the minimum term prescribed upon a first conviction as a minimum
    D. with a maximum of not more than twice the longest term prescribed for a first conviction for this crime

22. According to the above paragraph, if the term for this crime for a first offender is up to three years, the possible indeterminate term for this crime as a second or third felony shall have a _____ of not _____ than _____ years.   22.____

    A. minimum; less; five
    B. maximum; more; five
    C. minimum; less; one and one-half
    D. maximum; less; six

23. A statute states: *A person who steals an article worth $1,000 or less where no aggravating circumstances accompany the act is guilty of petit larceny. If the article is worth more than $1,000, it may be grand larceny.*   23.____
If all you know is that Edward Smith stole an article worth $1,000, it may reasonably be said that

    A. Smith is guilty of petit larceny
    B. Smith is guilty of grand larceny
    C. Smith is guilty of neither petit larceny nor grand larceny
    D. precisely what charge will be placed against Smith is uncertain

Questions 24-25.

DIRECTIONS: Questions 24 and 25 are to be answered on the basis of the following section of a law.

A person who, after having been three times convicted within this state of felonies or attempts to commit felonies, or under the law of any other state, government, or country, of crimes which if committed within this state would be felonious, commits a felony, other than murder, first or second degree, or treason, within this state, shall be sentenced upon conviction of such fourth, or subsequent, offense to imprisonment in a state prison for an indeterminate term the minimum of which shall be not less than the maximum term provided for first offenders for the crime for which the individual has been convicted, but, in any event, the minimum term upon conviction for a felony as the fourth or subsequent, offense shall be not less than fifteen years, and the maximum thereof shall be his natural life.

24. Under the terms of the above law, a person must receive the increased punishment therein provided if   24._____

    A. he is convicted of a felony and has been three times previously convicted of felonies

    B. he has been three times previously convicted of felonies, regardless of the nature of his present conviction

    C. his fourth conviction is for murder, first or second degree, or treason

    D. he has previously been convicted three times of murder, first or second degree, or treason

25. Under the terms of the above law, a person convicted of a felony for which the penalty is imprisonment for a term not to exceed ten years, and who has been three times previously convicted of felonies in this state, shall be sentenced to a term, the MINIMUM of which shall be   25._____

    A. 10 years   B. 15 years

    C. indeterminate   D. his natural life

———————

KEY (CORRECT ANSWERS)

1.	C		11.	A
2.	B		12.	B
3.	D		13.	A
4.	A		14.	B
5.	C		15.	B
6.	D		16.	B
7.	A		17.	C
8.	D		18.	D
9.	C		19.	C
10.	B		20.	A

21.	D
22.	C
23.	D
24.	A
25.	B

———

INTERPRETING STATISTICAL DATA
GRAPHS, CHARTS AND TABLES
EXAMINATION SECTION
TEST 1

DIRECTIONS: Each question or incomplete statement is followed by several suggested answers or completions. Select the one that BEST answers the question or completes the statement. *PRINT THE LETTER OF THE CORRECT ANSWER IN THE SPACE AT THE RIGHT.*

Questions 1-4.

DIRECTIONS: Questions 1 through 4 are to be answered SOLELY on the basis of the following table.

STOLEN AND RECOVERED PROPERTY IN COMMUNITY X				
2018-2019				
Type of Property	Value of Property Stolen		Value of Property Recovered	
	2018	2019	2018	2019
Currency	$264,925	$204,534	$10,579	$13,527
Jewelry	165,317	106,885	20,913	20,756
Furs	10,007	24,028	105	1,620
Clothing	62,265	49,219	4,322 7	15,821
Automobiles	740,719	606,062	36,701	558,442
Miscellaneous	356,901	351,064	62,077	103,117
TOTAL	$1,600,134	$1,341,792	$834,697	$713,283

1. Of the following types of property, the one which shows the HIGHEST ratio of *value of property recovered* to *value of property stolen* is

    A. clothing for 2018
    C. jewelry for 2019
    B. currency for 2018
    D. miscellaneous for 2019

1.____

2. Of the types of property which show a decrease from 2018 to 2019 in the value of property stolen, the one which shows the GREATEST percentage decrease in the value of the property recovered is

    A. automobiles
    C. furs
    B. currency
    D. jewelry

2.____

3. According to the above table, the total value of currency and jewelry stolen in 2019, as compared to 2018, decreased APPROXIMATELY by

    A. 3%   B. 20%   C. 28%   D. 38%

3.____

4. According to the above table, the TOTAL value of all types of property recovered was 4.____

    A. a slightly lower percentage of the value of property stolen for 2018 than for 2019

    B. less for the year 2018 than the value of any individual type of property recovered for the year 2019

    C. approximately 60% of the value of all property stolen in 2018 and approximately 70% in 2019

    D. greater for the year 2019 than the value of any individual type of property recovered for the year 2018

KEY (CORRECT ANSWERS)

    1. D
    2. A
    3. C
    4. A

TEST 2

Questions 1-6.

DIRECTIONS: Questions 1 through 6 are to be answered SOLELY on the basis of the information supplied in the chart below.

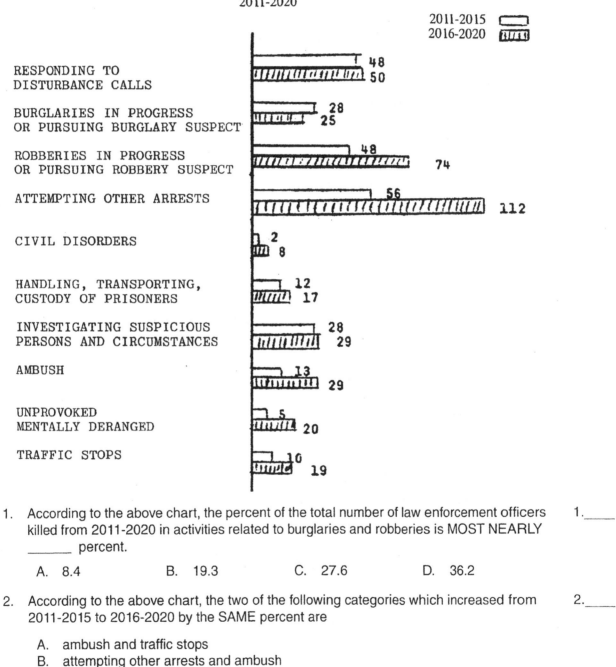

LAW ENFORCEMENT OFFICERS KILLED
(By Type of Activity)
2011-2020

2011-2015
2016-2020

RESPONDING TO DISTURBANCE CALLS — 48 / 50

BURGLARIES IN PROGRESS OR PURSUING BURGLARY SUSPECT — 28 / 25

ROBBERIES IN PROGRESS OR PURSUING ROBBERY SUSPECT — 48 / 74

ATTEMPTING OTHER ARRESTS — 56 / 112

CIVIL DISORDERS — 2 / 8

HANDLING, TRANSPORTING, CUSTODY OF PRISONERS — 12 / 17

INVESTIGATING SUSPICIOUS PERSONS AND CIRCUMSTANCES — 28 / 29

AMBUSH — 13 / 29

UNPROVOKED MENTALLY DERANGED — 5 / 20

TRAFFIC STOPS — 10 / 19

1. According to the above chart, the percent of the total number of law enforcement officers killed from 2011-2020 in activities related to burglaries and robberies is MOST NEARLY _____ percent.

   A. 8.4   B. 19.3   C. 27.6   D. 36.2

2. According to the above chart, the two of the following categories which increased from 2011-2015 to 2016-2020 by the SAME percent are

   A. ambush and traffic stops
   B. attempting other arrests and ambush

C. civil disorders and unprovoked mentally deranged
D. response to disturbance calls and investigating suspicious persons and circumstances

3. According to the above chart, the percentage increase in law enforcement officers killed
from the 2011-2015 period to the 2016-2020 period is MOST NEARLY _____ percent.

   A. 34   B. 53   C. 65   D. 100

3.____

4. According to the above chart, in which one of the following activities did the number of
law enforcement officers killed increase by 100 percent?

   A. Ambush
   B. Attempting other arrests
   C. Robberies in progress or pursuing robbery suspect
   D. Traffic stops

4.____

5. According to the above chart, the two of the following activities during which the total
number of law enforcement officers killed from 2011 to 2020 was the SAME are

   A. burglaries in progress or pursuing burglary suspect and investigating suspicious
persons and circumstances
   B. handling, transporting, custody of prisoners and traffic stops
   C. investigating suspicious persons and circumstances and ambush
   D. responding to disturbance calls and robberies in progress or pursuing robbery sus-
pect

5.____

6. According to the categories in the above chart, the one of the following statements which
can be made about law enforcement officers killed from 2011 to 2015 is that

   A. the number of law enforcement officers killed during civil disorders equals one-
sixth of the number killed responding to disturbance calls
   B. the number of law enforcement officers killed during robberies in progress or pursuing robbery suspect equals 25 percent of the number killed while handling or
transporting prisoners
   C. the number of law enforcement officers killed during traffic stops equals one-half
the number killed for unprovoked reasons or by the mentally deranged
   D. twice as many law enforcement officers were killed attempting other arrests as
were killed during burglaries in progress or pursuing burglary suspect

6.____

KEY (CORRECT ANSWERS)

1. C
2. C
3. B
4. B
5. B
6. D

TEST 3

Questions 1-6.

DIRECTIONS: Questions 1 through 6 are to be answered SOLELY on the basis of the graph below.

YEARLY INCIDENCE OF MAJOR CRIMES FOR COMMUNITY Z
2017-2019

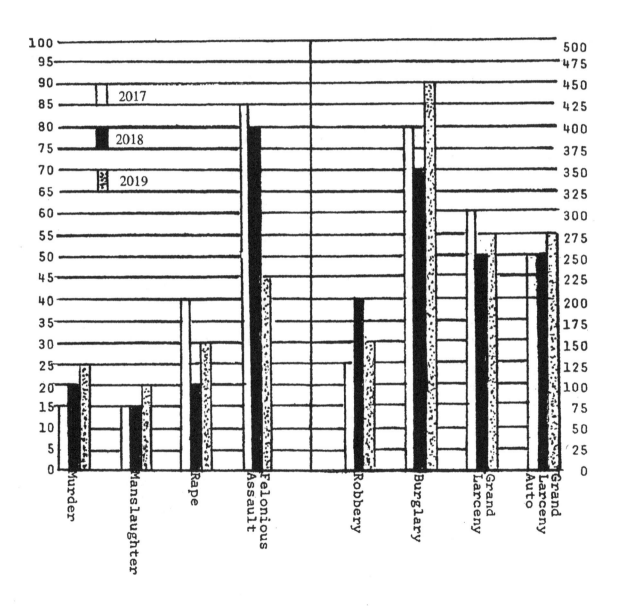

CRIMES AGAINST THE PERSON   CRIMES AGAINST PROPERTY

1. Of the following crimes, the one for which the 2019 figure was GREATER than the average of the previous two years was

    A. grand larceny   B. manslaughter
    C. rape   D. robbery

1.____

2. If the incidence of burglary in 2020 were to increase over 2019 by the same number as it increased in 2019 over 2018, then the average for this crime for the four-year period from 2017 through 2020 would be MOST NEARLY

    A. 100   B. 400   C. 415   D. 440

2.____

3. The above graph indicates that the percentage INCREASE in grand larceny auto over the previous year was

    A. greater in 2019 than in 2018
    B. greater in 2018 than in 2019
    C. greater in 2019 than in 2017
    D. the same in both 2018 and 2019

3.____

4. The one of the following which cannot be determined because there is not enough information in the above graph to do so is the

    A. percentage of *Crimes Against Property* for the three-year period which were committed in 2017
    B. percentage of *Crimes Against the Person* for the three-year period which were murders committed in 2018
    C. percentage of *Major Crimes* for the three-year period which were committed in the first six months of 2018
    D. major crimes which were following a pattern of continuing yearly increases for the three-year period

4.____

5. According to this graph, the ratio of *Crimes Against Property* to *Crimes Against the Person* for 2019, as compared to the ratio for 2018, is

    A. increasing   B. decreasing
    C. about the same   D. cannot be determined

5.____

6. Assume that it is desired to present information from the above graph to the public in a form most likely to gain their cooperation in a special police effort to reduce the incidence of grand larceny auto.
The one of the following which is MOST likely to result in such cooperation is a public statement that

    A. in 2019, approximately .75 of an automobile was stolen every day
    B. in 2019, one automobile was stolen, on the average, about,32 hours hours
    C. the number of automobiles stolen per year will increase from year to year
    D. there were more crimes of grand larceny auto than crimes of robbery committed during the past three years

6.____

KEY (CORRECT ANSWERS)

1.	B	4.	C
2.	D	5.	A
3.	B	6.	B

TEST 4

Questions 1-7.

DIRECTIONS: Questions 1 through 7 are to be answered SOLELY on the basis of the information contained in the following tables and chart.

TABLE 1

Number of Murders by Region, United States: 2014 and 2015

Region	Year	
	2014	2015
Northeastern States	2,521	2,849
North Central States	3,427	3,697
Southern States	6,577	7,055
Western States	2,062	2,211

Number in each case for given year and region represents total number (100%) of murders in that region for that year.

TABLE 2

Murder by Circumstance, U.S. - 2015
(Percent distribution by category)

Region	Total	Spouse Killing spouse	Parent Killing child	Other family killings	Romantic triangle and lovers' quarrels	Other arguments	Known Felony type	Suspected felony type
Northeastern States	100.0	9.6	3.7	6.1	7.9	38.4	25.4	8.9
North Central States	100.0	11.3	3.0	8.9	5.0	39.5	22.4	9.9
Southern States	100.0	13.8	2.2	8.8	8.4	46.0	13.9	6.9
Western States	100.0	12.5	4.9	7.0	6.4	32.2	28.0	9.0

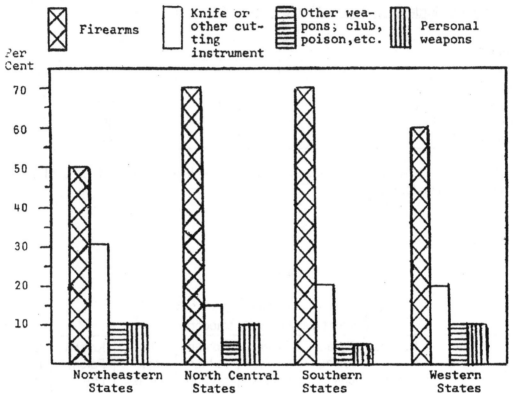

CHART 1

Murder by Type of Weapon Used, U.S. - 2015
(Percent Distribution)

1. The number of persons murdered by firearms in the Western States in 2015 was MOST   1.___
    NEARLY

    A. 220   B. 445   C. 1235   D. 1325

2. In 2015, the number of murders in the category *Parent killing child* was GREATEST in   2.___
    the _____ States.

    A. Northeastern   B. North Central
    C. Southern   D. Western

3. The difference between the number of persons murdered with firearms and the number   3.___
    of persons murdered with other weapons (club, poison, etc.) in the North Central States
    in 2015 is MOST NEARLY

    A. 2200   B. 2400   C. 2600   D. 2800

4. In 2014, the ratio of the number of murders in the Western States to the total number of   4.___
    murders in the U.S. was MOST NEARLY

    A. 1 to 4   B. 1 to 5   C. 1 to 7   D. 1 to 9

5. The total number of murders in the U.S. in the category of *Romantic triangles and lovers'* *quarrels* in 2015 was MOST NEARLY   5.____

    A. 850   B. 950   C. 1050   D. 1150

6. Which of the following represents the GREATEST number of murders in 2015?   6.____
Persons murdered by

    A. firearms in the Western States
    B. knives or other cutting instruments in the Southern States
    C. knives or other cutting instruments and persons murdered by other weapons (club, poison, etc.) in the Northeastern States
    D. knives or other cutting instruments, persons murdered by other weapons (club, poison, etc.) and persons murdered by personal weapons in the North Central States

7. From 2014 to 2015, the total number of murders increased by the GREATEST percentage in the _____ States.   7.____

    A. Northeastern   B. North Central
    C. Southern   D. Western

KEY (CORRECT ANSWERS)

    1. D
    2. C
    3. B
    4. C
    5. D
    6. B
    7. A

TEST 5

Questions 1-5.

DIRECTIONS: Questions 1 through 5 are to be answered SOLELY on the basis of the following.

DISTRIBUTION OF CITIZENS' RESPONSES TO STATEMENTS
CONCERNING SHERIFFS' ARRESTS
(Number of citizens responding = 1171)

	CATEGORIES				
	(A) Strongly Agree	(B) Agree	(C) Disagree	(D) Strongly Disagree	(E) Don't Know
I. Sheriffs act improperly in arresting defendants, even when these persons are rude and ill-mannered	12%	37%	36%	9%	6%
II. Sheriffs frequently use more force than necessary when making arrests	9%	19%	46%	19%	7%
III. Any defendant who insults or physically abuses a sheriff has no complaint if he is sternly handled in return	13%	44%	32%	7%	4%

1. The total percentage of responses to Statement III OTHER THAN *Strongly Agree* and *Disagree* is   1.____

    A. 45%   B. 46%   C. 55%   D. 59%

2. The number of *Disagree* responses to Statement II is MOST NEARLY '   2.____

    A. 71   B. 114   C. 539   D. 820

3. Assume that for Statement II the (B) percentage of responses were doubled and the (A) percentage increased one and a half times.
If the (D) and (E) percentages remained the same, the (C) percentage would then MOST NEARLY be

    A. 23%   B. 26%   C. 39%   D. 52%

3.____

4. The total number of *Don't Know* responses is MOST NEARLY

    A. 17
    B. 188
    C. 200
    D. a figure which cannot be determined from the table

4.____

5. If the percentage of Disagree responses to Statement III were 35% less, the resulting percentage would MOST NEARLY be

    A. 11%   B. 14%   C. 15%   D. 21%

5.____

KEY (CORRECT ANSWERS)

1. C
2. C
3. A
4. C
5. D

TEST 6

Questions 1-3.

DIRECTIONS: Questions 1 through 3 are to be answered SOLELY on the basis of the statistical report given below.

The following is a statistical report of the activities of the bureau during the current year as compared with the previous year.

	Current Year	Previous Year
Memoranda of law prepared	68	83
Legal matters forwarded to Corporation Counsel	122	144
Letters requesting legal information	756	807
Letters requesting departmental records	139	111
Matters for publication	17	26
Court appearances of members of bureau	4,678	4,621
Conferences	94	103
Lectures at Police Academy	30	33
Reports on proposed legislation	194	255
Deciphering of codes	79	27
Expert testimony	31	16
Notices to court witnesses	55	81
Briefs prepared	22	18
Court papers prepared	258	

1. According to the report, the percentage of bills prepared and sponsored by the Legal Bureau which were passed by the State Legislature and sent to the Governor for approval was APPROXIMATELY

   A.   3.1%
   B.   2.6%
   C.   .5%
   D.   not capable of determination from the data given

1.____

2. According to the statistical report, the activity showing the GREATEST percentage of *decrease* in the current year as compared with the previous year was

   A.   matters for publication
   B.   reports on proposed legislation

2.____

   C.   notices to court witnesses
   D.   memoranda of law prepared

3. According to the statistical report, the activity showing the GREATEST percentage of   3._____
    increase in the current year as compared with the previous year was

   A.   court appearances of members of the bureau
   B.   giving expert testimony
   C.   deciphering of codes
   D.   letters requesting departmental records

KEY (CORRECT ANSWERS)

   1.   D
   2.   A
   3.   C

TEST 7

Questions 1-5.

DIRECTIONS: Questions 1 through 5 are to be answered SOLELY on the basis of the information contained in Tables I and II that appear below and on the following page.

TABLE I
NUMBER OF ARRESTS FOR VARIOUS CRIMES AND DISPOSITION

OFFENSES	TOTAL ARRESTED	INVESTIGATED AND RELEASED	HELD FOR PROSECUTION	GUILTY AS CHARGED	GUILTY OF LESSER OFFENSES	DISPOSITION OTHER THAN CONVICTION
Murder	48	10	38	12	9	17
Rape	41	10	31	8	3	20
Aggravated assault	241	106	135	36	32	67
Robbery	351	177	174	98	35	41
Burglary	890	371	519	322	88	109
Larceny	1,665	466 78	1,199	929	58	212
Auto theft	464		386	278	46	62
TOTAL	3,700	1,218	2,482	1,683	271	528

TABLE II

ARRESTS FOR LARCENY - PERCENTAGE OF SUCH ARRESTS BY AGE AND SEX

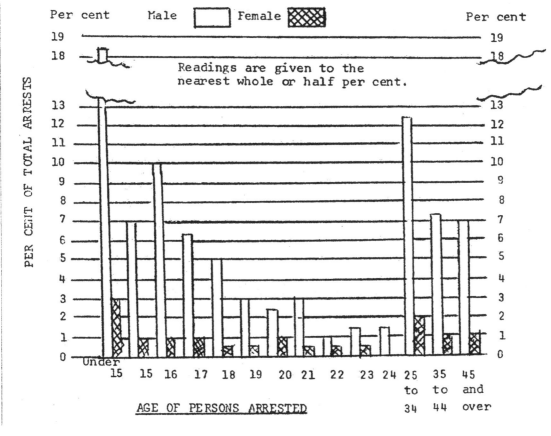

1. The category in which the HIGHEST percentage of those arrested were found guilty as charged was

    A. robbery   B. burglary   C. larceny   D. auto theft

    1.____

2. The number of 21-year-olds, both males and females, arrested for larceny is MOST NEARLY

    A. 29   B. 37   C. 42   D. 58

    2.____

3. The total number of males arrested for larceny, as compared to the number of females arrested for larceny, is _____ times as great.

    A. 5   B. 6   C. 8   D. 10

    3.____

4. Considering only the category of larceny, the one of the following statements which is INCORRECT is:

    A. The percentage of 25-year-old males arrested cannot be determined
    B. Twice as many 16-year-old males were arrested as 18-year-old males

    4.____

C. The percentage of 16-year-old males arrested was twice as high as the percentage of 18-year-old males

D. Persons 19 years of age and younger accounted for exactly half of the total arrests for larceny

5. The one of the following which is the MOST accurate statement with respect to the disposition of arrests in each category is that in   5.____

A. no category was the number investigated and released greater than half the number arrested

B. no category was the number investigated and released less than one-fifth of those arrested

C. only two categories was the number found guilty of lesser offense greater than one-tenth of those arrested

D. only one category was the number found guilty as charged less than one-fourth of those arrested

---

KEY (CORRECT ANSWERS)

1. D
2. D
3. B
4. D
5. C

TEST 8

Questions 1-5.

DIRECTIONS: Questions 1 through 5 are to be answered SOLELY on the basis of the table below.

VALUE OF PROPERTY STOLEN - 2017 AND 2018
LARCENY

Category	2017		2018	
	Number of Offenses	Value of Stolen Property	Number of Offense	Value of Stolen Property
Pocket -picking	20	$1,950	10	$ 950
Purse- snatching	175	5,750	20	12,500
Shoplifting	155	7,950	225	17,350
Automobile thefts	1,040	127,050	860	108,000
Thefts of auto accessories	1,135	34,950	970	24,400
Bicycle thefts	355	8,250	240	6,350
All other thefts	1,375	187,150	1,300	153,150

1. Of the total number of larcenies reported for 2017, automobile thefts accounted for MOST NEARLY   1.____

    A. 5%   B.   15%   C.   25%   D.   50%

2. The LARGEST percentage decrease in the value of the stolen property from 2017 to 2018 was in the category of   2.____

    A. pocket-picking
    B. automobile thefts
    C. thefts of automobile accessories
    D. bicycle thefts

3. In 2018, the average amount of each theft was LOWEST for the category of   3.____

    A. pocket-picking
    B. purse-snatching
    C. shoplifting
    D. thefts of auto accessories

4. The category which had the LARGEST numerical reduction in the number of offenses from 2017 to 2018 was   4.____

    A. pocket-picking
    B. automobile thefts
    C. thefts of auto accessories
    D. bicycle thefts

5. When the categories are ranked for each year according to the number of offenses com-   5.____
   mitted in each category (largest number to rank first), the number of categories which will
   have the SAME rank in 2017 as in 2018 is

   A.   3   B.   4   C.   5   D.   6

KEY (CORRECT ANSWERS)

1.   C
2.   A
3.   D
4.   B
5.   C

TEST 9

Questions 1-5.

DIRECTIONS: Questions 1 through 5 are to be answered SOLELY on the basis of the graphs below.

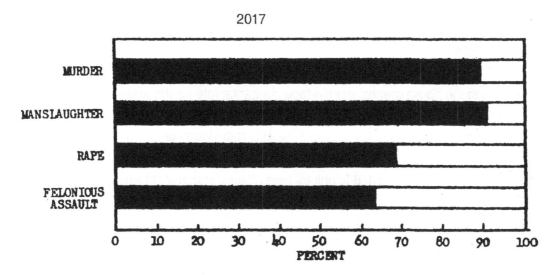

2017

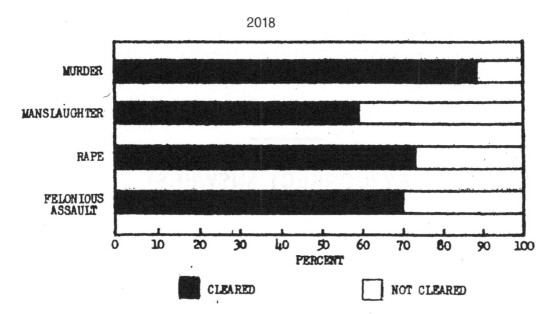

2018

CLEARED   NOT CLEARED

NOTE: The clearance rate is defined as the percentage of reported cases which were closed by the police through arrests or other means.

1. According to the above graphs, the AVERAGE clearance rate for all four crimes for 2018   1._____

    A. was greater than in 2017
    B. was less than in 2017

    C.   was the same as in 2017
    D.   cannot properly be compared to the 2017 figures

2. According to the above graphs, the crimes which did NOT show an increasing clearance   2.____
    rate from 2017 to 2018 were

    A.   manslaughter and murder
    B.   rape and felonious assault
    C.   manslaughter and felonious assault
    D.   rape and murder

3. According to the above graphs, the average clearance rate for the two-year period 2017-   3.____
    2018 was SMALLEST for the crime of

    A.   murder   B.   manslaughter
    C.   rape   D.   felonious assault

4. If, in 2018, 63 cases of reported felonious assault remained *not cleared,* then the total   4.____
    number of felonious assault cases reported that year was MOST NEARLY

    A. 90   B.   150   C.   210   D.   900

5. In comparing the graphs for 2017 and 2018, it would be MOST accurate to state that   5.____

    A.   it is not possible to compare the total number of crimes cleared in 2017 with the
         total number cleared in 2018
    B.   the total number of crimes reported in 2017 is greater than the number in 2018
    C.   there were fewer manslaughter cases cleared during 2017 than in 2018
    D.   there were more rape cases cleared during 2018 than manslaughter cases cleared
         in the same year

_____

KEY (CORRECT ANSWERS)

1. B
2. A
3. D
4. C
5. A

_____

TEST 10

Questions 1-5.

DIRECTIONS: Questions 1 through 5 are to be answered SOLELY on the basis of the following chart.

FATAL HIGHWAY ACCIDENTS						
	Drivers Over 18 Years of Age			Drivers 18 Years of Age And Under		
2018	Auto	Other Vehicles	Total	Auto	Other Vehicles	Total
January	43	0	43	4	0	4
February	52	0	52	10	0	10
March	36	0	36	8	0	8
April	50	0	50	17	0	17
May	40	2	42	5	0	5
June	26	0	26	8	0	8
July	29	0	29	6	0	6
August	29	1	30	3	0	3
September	36	0	36	4	0	4
October	45	1	46	2	1	3
November	54	1	55	3	0	3
December	66	1	67	3	0	6
TOTALS	506	6	512	76	1	77

1. The average number of fatal auto accidents per month during 2018 involving drivers older than eighteen was MOST NEARLY

   A. 42   B. 43   C. 44   D. 45

1.____

2. The TOTAL number of fatal highway accidents during 2018 was

   A. 506   B. 512   C. 582   D. 589

2.____

3. The month during which the LOWEST number of fatal highway accidents occurred was

   A. March   B. June   C. July   D. August

3.____

4. Of the total number of fatal highway accidents during 2018 involving drivers older than eighteen, the percentage of accidents which took place during December is MOST NEARLY

    A. 10   B. 13   C. 16   D. 19

4.____

5. The GREATEST percentage drop in fatal highway accidents occurred from

    A. February to March   B. April to May
    C. June to July   D. July to Augus

5.____

————

KEY (CORRECT ANSWERS)

1. A
2. D
3. D
4. B
5. B

————

EXAMINATION SECTION
TEST 1

DIRECTIONS: Each question or incomplete statement is followed by several suggested answers or completions. Select the one that BEST answers the question or completes the statement. *PRINT THE CORRECT ANSWER IN THE SPACE AT THE RIGHT.*

1. The OPPOSITE of familiar is   1.____

    A. friendly   B. old   C. strange
    D. aloof   E. different

2. If 4 pencils cost 10 cents, how many pencils can be bought for 50 cents?   2.____

3. A man does not always have   3.____

    A. arteries   B. hair   C. muscle
    D. skin   E. blood

4. What letter in the word *Washington* is the same number in the word (counting from the beginning) as it is in the alphabet?   4.____

5. tests children intelligence hundreds have of taken If the above words were arranged to make the best sentence, the LAST word of the sentence would begin with what letter? (Make it like a printed capital.)   5.____

6. A word meaning the same as change is   6.____

    A. endure   B. cause   C. result
    D. alter   E. anticipate

7. Copper is cheaper than gold because it is   7.____

    A. duller   B. more plentiful   C. harder
    D. uglier   E. less useful

8. An egg is related to a bird in the same way that a _____ is related to a plant.   8.____

    A. shell   B. leaf   C. root
    D. feather   E. seed

9. If 10 boxes full of oranges weigh 600 pounds and each box when empty weighs 6 pounds, how many pounds do all the oranges weigh?   9.____

10. The OPPOSITE of skillful is   10.____

    A. lazy   B. clumsy   C. weak
    D. slow   E. novice

Questions 11-13.

DIRECTIONS: Answer Questions 11 through 13 by choosing the CORRECT proverb meaning given below.

    A. A conscientious worker needs no prodding.
    B. Geese that lay golden eggs are too tough to eat.

C. In dire distress, any aid is acceptable.
D. Don't destroy the things that do you good.
E. A willing horse should be whipped lightly.
F. Ships should not venture out to sea in stormy weather.

11. Which statement above explains the proverb, *Kill not the goose that lays the golden eggs?*   11._____

12. Which statement above explains the proverb, *Any port in a storm?*   12._____

13. Which statement above explains the proverb, *Don't spur a willing horse?*   13._____

14. In general, it is safer to judge a woman's character by her   14._____

    A. face   B. cooking   C. clothes
    D. deeds   E. speeches

15. An ellipse is related to a circle as a diamond is to a   15._____

    A. ring   B. square   C. rectangle
    D. oval   E. cube

16. A mare is always _____ than her colt.   16._____

    A. faster   B. sleeker   C. bigger
    D. older   E. stronger

17. The OPPOSITE of wasteful is   17._____

    A. wealthy   B. quiet   C. stingy
    D. economical   E. extravagant

18. 1   5   2   6   3   7   4   9   5   9   18._____
One number is wrong in the above series.
What should that number be?

19. Such things as looks, dress, likes, and dislikes indicate one's   19._____

    A. character   B. wisdom   C. personality
    D. gossip   E. reputation

20. A picnic consisted of a minister, six deacons and their wives, and three children in each of the deacons' families. How many were there at the picnic?   20._____

21. At a dinner there is ALWAYS   21._____

    A. soup   B. wine   C. food
    D. waiters   E. dishes

22. The idea that the earth is flat is   22._____

    A. absurd   B. misleading   C. improbable
    D. unfair   E. wicked

23. Which word is needed to begin the following sentence?   23._____
_____ a geometrical figure has three straight sides, it is a triangle.

    A. Although   B. If   C. Since
    D. Now that   E. Because

24. All residents in this block are Republicans.
Smith is not a Republican.
Smith resides in this block.
If the first two statements are true, the third is

    A.   true   B.   false   C.   not certain

24.____

25. The OPPOSITE of seldom is

    A.   never   B.   many   C.   invariably
    D.   always   E.   frequently

25.____

KEY (CORRECT ANSWERS)

1.	C	11.	D
2.	20	12.	C
3.	B	13.	A
4.	G	14.	D
5.	T	15.	B
6.	D	16.	D
7.	B	17.	D
8.	E	18.	8
9.	540	19.	C
10.	B	20.	31

21.	C
22.	A
23.	B
24.	B
25.	E

TEST 2

DIRECTIONS: Each question or incomplete statement is followed by several suggested answers or completions. Select the one that BEST answers the question or completes the statement. *PRINT THE CORRECT ANSWER IN THE SPACE AT THE RIGHT.*

1. Which one of these things is MOST unlike the other four?   1.____

    A. Bean   B. Cherry   C. Pea   D. Carrot   E. Beet

2. A sewing machine is related to a needle as a typewriter is to   2.____

    A. a pin   B. a cloth   C. ink
    D. a pen   E. a page

3. The two words *repentant* and *reluctant* mean   3.____

    A. the same
    B. the opposite
    C. neither same nor opposite

4. The OPPOSITE of brave is   4.____

    A. intrepid   B. weak   C. treacherous
    D. cowardly   E. fragile

5. Z F Z S E Y Z F S Y F Z F F S Y S Z F E Z F S F Z Y F Z F Y   5.____
Count each Z in this series that is followed by an F next to it if the F is now followed by an S next to it.
Tell how many Z's you count.

6. If a boy can run 2 feet in 1/10 of a second, how many feet can he run in 10 seconds?   6.____

Questions 7-9.

DIRECTIONS: Answer Questions 7 through 9 by choosing the CORRECT proverb meaning given below.

    A. Chickens are easier to count than eggs.
    B. People tend to associate with others like themselves.
    C. Prying into the affairs of others may bring trouble.
    D. Birds fly in large flocks.
    E. Don't rely too much on your anticipations.
    F. Cats are often too curious.

7. Which statement above explains the proverb, *Curiosity killed the cat?*   7.____

8. Which statement above explains the proverb, *Don't count your chickens before they are hatched?*   8.____

9. Which statement above explains the proverb, *Birds of a feather flock together?*   9.____

10. best hard road the work success to is   10.____
If the above words were arranged to make a good sentence, the FOURTH word of the sentence would begin with what letter?

11. Frank is older than George.
    James is older than Frank.
    George is younger than James.
    If the first two statements are true, the third is

    A. true   B. false   C. not certain

    11._____

12. One who says things he knows to be wrong is said to be

    A. careless   B. misled   C. conceited
    D. untruthful   E. prejudiced

    12._____

13. The OPPOSITE of create is

    A. sustain   B. evolution   C. transform
    D. explode   E. abolish

    13._____

14. If $3\frac{1}{2}$ yards of cloth cost $9, how many dollars will 7 yards cost?

    14._____

15. Which of the five things following is MOST unlike the other four?

    A. Nail   B. Hammer   C. Screw
    D. Bolt   E. Tack

    15._____

16. Darkness is to sunlight as _____ is to sound.

    A. noise   B. brightness   C. air
    D. echo   E. quiet

    16._____

17. The OPPOSITE of gentle is

    A. strong   B. careless   C. humane
    D. thoughtless   E. rough

    17._____

18. Some members of this club are Baptists.
    Some members of this club are lawyers.
    Some members of this club are Baptist lawyers.
    If the first two statements above are true, the third is

    A. true   B. false   C. not certain

    18._____

19. If $4\frac{1}{2}$ yards of cloth cost 90 cents, how many cents will $3\frac{1}{2}$ yards cost?

    19._____

20. A line is to a point as a surface is to

    A. flat   B. line   C. solid   D. square   E. plane

    20._____

21. The two words *precise* and *indefinite* mean

    A. the same
    B. the opposite
    C. neither same nor opposite

    21._____

22. When two windows have the same shape, the dimensions of one are _____ the dimen-   22.____
    sions of the other.

    A. equal to   B. greater than
    C. less than   D. proportional to
    E. double

23. Suppose that the first and second letters of the alphabet were interchanged, also the   23.____
    third and fourth, the fifth and sixth, etc.
    Write the letter which would then be the sixteenth letter of the series.

24. If a strip of cloth 32 inches long will shrink to 28 inches when washed, how many inches   24.____
    long will a 48-inch strip be after shrinking?

25. Which one of the following five words is MOST unlike the other four?   25.____

    A. Was   B. Came   C. Have   D. Stay   E. Here

———————

KEY (CORRECT ANSWERS)

1.	B		11.	A
2.	D		12.	D
3.	C		13.	E
4.	D		14.	18
5.	4		15.	B
6.	200		16.	E
7.	C		17.	E
8.	E		18.	C
9.	B		19.	70
10.	T		20.	E

21.	B
22.	D
23.	O
24.	42
25.	E

———————

TEST 3

DIRECTIONS: Each question or incomplete statement is followed by several suggested answers or completions. Select the one that BEST answers the question or completes the statement. *PRINT THE CORRECT ANSWER IN THE SPACE AT THE RIGHT.*

1. A city ALWAYS has   1.____

   A. street cars   B. a mayor
   C. traffic officers   D. residents
   E. churches

2. A word meaning the same as congratulate is   2.____

   A. felicitate   B. commemorate   C. reward
   D. console   E. promote

3. Find the two letters in the word *canal* which have just as many letters between them in   3.____
   the word as in the alphabet. Write the one of these two letters that comes FIRST in the
   alphabet.

4. The mandates of a dictator are   4.____

   A. obsolete   B. arbitrary   C. omnipotent
   D. conditional   E. optional

5. Which one of the five words below is MOST like these three: love, hate, joy?   5.____

   A. Memory   B. Taste   C. Anger
   D. Health   E. Life

6. A gulf is to the ocean as a _____ is to a continent.   6.____

   A. mountain   B. river   C. land
   D. peninsula   E. island

7. A B C D E F G H I J K L M N O P Q R S T U V W X Y Z   7.____
   If all the even-numbered letters in the alphabet were crossed out, the TWELFTH letter
   left not crossed out would be what letter?

8. Write the letter of the alphabet which is the third to the right of the letter which is midway   8.____
   between O and S.

9. A hotel serves a mixture of 2 parts cream and 3 parts milk.   9.____
   How many pints of milk will it take to make 15 pints of the mixture?

10. Which of the following is a trait of character?   10.____

    A. Reputation   B. Wealth   C. Influence
    D. Fickleness   E. Strength

11. A man who spends his money lavishly for non-essentials is considered to be   11.____

    A. fortunate   B. thrifty   C. extravagant
    D. generous   E. economical

12. 1 4 9 16 25 36 45 64   12.____
    One number is wrong in the above series.
    What should that number be?

13. Democracy is to monarchy as corporation is to   13.____

    A. board of directors
    B. stockholders
    C. partnership
    D. general manager
    E. individual enterprise

14. How many of the following words can be made of the letters in the word *celebrate,* using   14.____
any letter twice: create, better, traceable, erect, tattle, rabble, crated, prattle, barter?

15. If George can ride a bicycle 60 feet while Frank runs 40 feet, how many feet can George   15.____
ride while Frank runs 60 feet?

16. choose care man A friends should with his If the above words were arranged to make a   16.____
good sentence, the FIFTH word in the sentence would begin with what letter?

17. It takes a good sense of balance to become a tight-rope walker.   17.____
John has a good sense of balance.
John will become a tight-rope walker.
If the first two statements above are true, the third is

    A. true   B. false   C. not certain

18. If a wire 40 inches long is to be cut so that one piece is 2/3 as long as the other piece,   18.____
how many inches must the longer piece be?

19. Find the letter which in this sentence itself appears a third time nearest the beginning.   19.____

20. Which of the following five things is MOST like these three: cotton, show, ivory?   20.____

    A. Soot   B. Milk   C. Ice   D. Ebony   E. Water

21. 1 2 4 7 11 16 22 28   21.____
One number is wrong in the above series.
What should that number be?

Questions 22-24.

DIRECTIONS: Questions 22 through 24 are to be answered on the basis of the following figure.

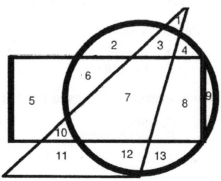

22. What number is in the space which is in the rectangle but not in the triangle or in the circle?　22.____

23. What number is in the same geometrical figure or figures (and no others) as the number 12?　23.____

24. How many spaces are there which are in any one but only one geometrical figure?　24.____

25. The OPPOSITE of *because* is　25.____

    A.　but　　　B.　since　　　C.　hence　　　D.　for　　　E.　and

KEY (CORRECT ANSWERS)

1.	D		11.	C
2.	A		12.	49
3.	L		13.	E
4.	B		14.	6
5.	C		15.	90
6.	D		16.	H
7.	W		17.	C
8.	T		18.	24
9.	9		19.	T
10.	D		20.	B

21.	29
22.	5
23.	6
24.	6
25.	A

EXAMINATION SECTION
TEST 1

DIRECTIONS: Each question or incomplete statement is followed by several suggested answers or completions. Select the one that BEST answers the question or completes the statement. *PRINT THE CORRECT ANSWER IN THE SPACE AT THE RIGHT.*

1. $75 \div \frac{1}{2} =$

1._____

2. LOCOMOTIVE is to TRACKS as AUTOMOBILE is to

2._____

    A. tires   B. gas   C. chauffeur
    D. road   E. motor

3. A VAGUE statement is

3._____

    A. clear   B. frank   C. impudent
    D. cross   E. uncertain

4. A DISCREPANCY is a(n)

4._____

    A. omission   B. order   C. disagreement
    D. misdemeanor   E. change

5. The HICKERY tree has tough wood.
The word in capitals is misspelled. Write it correctly at the right.

5._____

6. Add: $27\frac{1}{4}$

      143 3/8

       $7\frac{1}{2}$

      ‾‾‾‾‾‾‾

6._____

7. Multiply: 8.309
           11.01

7._____

8. Divide: .073)‾.365‾

8._____

9. NIGHT is to DAY as DARK is to

9._____

    A. black   B. stars   C. cold
    D. light   E. deep

10. A SLUGGISH stream is

10._____

    A. swift   B. dirty   C. muddy
    D. slow   E. active

11. A PITCHER is

11._____

    A. something used on the table

    B.   a useful article
    C.   a container for liquids
    D.   easily broken
    E.   a painting

12.   100 pounds were added to the WAYT of each load.
      The word in capitals is misspelled. Write it correctly at the right.

                                                       12.____

13.   If you can travel $\frac{1}{2}$ mile in one minute, how far can you travel in $\frac{1}{2}$ minute?   13.____

14.   Glass is valuable because it is   14.____

    A.   breakable   B.   thick
    C.   transparent   D.   protection against cold
    E.   insoluble

15.   A certain garden plot contains 27 tomato plants.   15.____
      If the length and width are doubled, how many plants will it contain?
      _____ as many.

    A.   Twice   B.   Three times   C.   Four times

16.   A LOOTENENT is an officer.   16.____
      The word in capitals is misspelled. Write it correctly at the right.

17.   How many square feet in a space 60 feet long and 10 feet wide?   17.____

18.   He was REKWESTED to leave.   18.____
      The word in capitals is misspelled. Write it correctly at the right.

19.   Canaries are kept in homes because they are   19.____

    A.   useful   B.   cheap
    C.   amusing   D.   used for food

20.   PEN is to INK as SOAP is to   20.____

    A.   hands   B.   clean   C.   water
    D.   suds   E.   odor

KEY (CORRECT ANSWERS)

1. 150
2. D
3. E
4. C
5. hickory

6. 178 1/8
7. 91.48209
8. E
9. D
10. D

11. C
12. weight
13. 1/4 mile
14. C
15. C

16. lieutenant
17. 600
18. requested
19. C
20. C

TEST 2

DIRECTIONS: Each question or incomplete statement is followed by several suggested answers or completions. Select the one that BEST answers the question or completes the statement. *PRINT THE CORRECT ANSWER IN THE SPACE AT THE RIGHT.*

1. Cut a 40 foot pole into 2 pieces, one 10 feet longer than the other. What is the length of the shorter piece? (If your answers are right, the shorter piece will be ten feet shorter than the longer.)

1.____

2. VELOCITY means MOST NEARLY

2.____

   A. wind   B. speed
   C. tricycle   D. sort of grass seed
   E. civic plan

3. To ADHERE means to

3.____

   A. hear easily   B. advertise   C. label
   D. be present   E. cling to

4. We traveled through three KUNTREES.
The word in capitals is misspelled. Write it correctly at the right.

4.____

5. IDENTICAL means

5.____

   A. to recognize   B. to bend   C. exactly alike
   D. nearly alike   E. an ignoramus

6. CASUALTY means

6.____

   A. a wreck   B. once in a while
   C. death by accident   D. insured
   E. slight

7. FISH are to WATER as BIRDS are to

7.____

   A. feathers   B. nests   C. flying
   D. trees   E. air   F. molting

8. DOZEN is to TWELVE as SCORE is to

8.____

   A. ten   B. fifty   C. eggs
   D. baseball   E. gross   F. twenty

9. There are 60 MINITZ in an hour.
The word in capitals is misspelled. Write it correctly at the right.

9.____

10. To be IMPARTIAL is

10.____

   A. to take sides   B. not to take sides
   C. to be unjust   D. to be in politics
   E. to give

11. We want to know the height of a certain pole. Its shadow is 20 feet long. The shadow of a yardstick is 2 feet long.
How high is the pole?

11._____

12. If you receive a 6% increase on your invested money, and you get $6.00 for 6 months interest, how much have you invested?

12._____

13. Which is taller, a boy 64 inches tall or a man 5 feet 3 inches?

13._____

14. SLOW is the opposite of

14._____

    A. gaining
    D. difficult
    B. smooth
    E. racing
    C. fast

15. CRUDE OIL

15._____

    A. is not refined
    C. is a varnish
    E. is heavy
    B. has bad odor
    D. is a plant

16. Sold an automobile for $125, thereby gaining 25%. Cost?

16._____

17. CAPITOL means

17._____

    A. money
    C. city
    E. tolling of bells
    B. punishment
    D. government building

18. If cigarettes are $1.50 a package, or 2 packages for $2.50, how many cigarettes would you get for $5.00? (20 cigarettes per package)

18._____

19. *The recent apparently increasing popularity of foolish endurance tests, such as bicycle riding, dancing, tree and flagpole sitting, suggests that those not taking, part in them are nevertheless being forced into one of their own—that of patient endurance of them.*
According to the above quotation, which one of the following statements is TRUE?

19._____

    A. These endurance tests prove scientific facts.
    B. These *contests* are losing popular interest.
    C. Dancing, tree and flagpole sitting contests are foolish.
    D. Those not taking part now will be forced to do so later.
    E. It is foolish to endure dancing or bicycle riding.

20. A train leaves at 10:50 A.M. and arrives at 4:26 P.M. It makes 9 stops of 4 minutes each. If it travels 50 miles an hour when running, how many miles did it cover?

20._____

KEY (CORRECT ANSWERS)

1.	15		11.	30
2.	B		12.	$200
3.	E		13.	boy
4.	countries		14.	C
5.	C		15.	A
6.	C		16.	$100
7.	E		17.	D
8.	F		18.	80
9.	minutes		19.	C
10.	B		20.	250

———

EXAMINATION SECTION
TEST 1

DIRECTIONS: Each question or incomplete statement is followed by several suggested answers or completions. Select the one that BEST answers the question or completes the statement. *PRINT THE CORRECT ANSWER IN THE SPACE AT THE RIGHT.*

1. One-half of all the mail is letters, one-third is cards, and the remainder consists of 300 papers.
   What is the TOTAL number of pieces in the mail?

   1.____

2. There are 5 dozen oranges and lemons in a basket. One-fifth of all the oranges equals the total number of lemons in the basket.
   How many lemons?

   2.____

3. DISIPLIN in the army is maintained always.
   The word in capitals is misspelled. Write it correctly at the right.

   3.____

4. We pledge ALEEJUNS to our flag.
   The word in capitals is misspelled. Write it correctly at the right.

   4.____

5. Cities pass laws to curb the smoke NYOOSANS.
   The word in capitals is misspelled. Write it correctly at the right.

   5.____

6. The policeman is PUTROHLING his beat.
   The word in capitals is misspelled. Write it correctly at the right.

   6.____

7. We are SEPURAYTING the good from the bad.
   The word in capitals is misspelled. Write it correctly at the right.

   7.____

8. Which one of the following words applies to LETTERS and MAGAZINES but not to MAIL CARRIER?

   8.____

   A. Authorized   B. Regular   C. Periodical
   D. Uniform   E. Mailed

9. *No doubt the most effective way of learning spelling is to train the eye carefully to observe the forms of the words we are reading. If this habit is formed and the habit of general reading accompanies it , it is sufficient to make a nearly perfect speller. However, the observation of the general form of a word is not the observation that teaches spelling. We must have the habit of observing every letter in every word, and this we are not likely to have unless we give special attention to acquiring it. Memory works by association. If we can work up a system which will serve the memory by way of association so that the slight effort that can be given in ordinary reading will serve to fix a word more or less fully, we can soon acquire a marvelous power in the accurate spelling of words.*

   9.____

   The above paragraph tells us that the MOST effective way of learning to spell accurately is to

   A. have good eyesight
   B. observe the general form of each word
   C. form the habit of reading
   D. observe every letter in every word
   E. memorize every word we read

10. Each book has 200 pages.
    In a set of books standing side by side on a shelf, how many pages are there between page 1 of Volume 1 and page 200 of Volume 2?

10.____

11. Joe can sort a bag of mail in 6 minutes. Al can sort a bag of mail in 12 minutes. How long will it take them to sort one bag of mail, working together?

11.____

12. THIS is to THAT as HERE is to

   A. where   B. when   C. what   D. there   E. how

12.____

13. X is to Z as A is to

   A. Y   B. C   C. alphabet
   D. letter   E. B

13.____

14. LETTER is to WORD as WORD is to

   A. alphabet   B. book   C. sentence
   D. spelling   E. chapter

14.____

15. To ISOLATE is to

   A. freeze   B. separate from others
   C. quarantine   D. be tardy often
   E. discipline

15.____

16. UNCOUTH means MOST NEARLY

   A. youthful   B. to straighten out
   C. boorish   D. masculine
   E. unhealthy

16.____

17. PERJURY means MOST NEARLY

   A. to swear out a warrant   B. to make a false oath
   C. to do things unlawfully   D. to commit a theft
   E. jury duty

17.____

18. Law-breakers are confined in a PENITENSHAREE.
    The word in capitals is misspelled. Write it correctly at the right.

18.____

19. Birds devour INKREDIBUL numbers of insects.
    The word in capitals is misspelled. Write it correctly at the right.

19.____

20. *The Federal Reserve System, by the pooling of resources, has provided a bulwark which is destined to prevent any public nervousness from manifesting itself in money panics. An example of its service in this respect occurred last winter. The failure of the Bank of the United States in New York City caused a run on currency. The banks turned to Federal Reserve System. Within a week or so, no less than a quarter of a billion dollars had been called for. Nobody would have heard of the incident but for its record in the publications of the Federal Reserve Bank of New York. In other days, such nervousness would have precipitated a panic of the dimensions of the ones we had in 1897 and in 1907. Judging from the above paragraph, it is TRUE that*

   A. exactly a quarter of a billion dollars is held in reserve by the United States
   B. the United States is deeply in debt

20.____

C. by pooling its resources the Federal Reserve System can definitely prevent money panics
D. in case of a run on currency, the Federal Reserve System would be helpless
E. public nervousness may bring on any conceivable emergency

21. *In the year of Washington's birth, another illustrious American, Benjamin Franklin, announced the forthcoming appearance of the first of a long series of POOR RICH-ARD'S ALMANACS. These quaint publications were famous for their homely maxims advocating industry and frugality. POOR RICHARD'S proverbs, however, preached more than pinch-penny policies. They taught wise spending as well as wise saving. They counseled that neither time, energy, nor money be spent except for that which well repays its cost in real value received. By converting thousands of readers to this homely philosophy, they had a profound and lasting effect on American social and business life. POOR RICHARD'S proverbs had a profound effect on Americans because they*

    21.____

    A. were published in Washington's time
    B. stated facts in a quaint manner
    C. helped to make Benjamin Franklin famous
    D. counseled wise spending, industry, and frugality
    E. suggested pinch-penny policies

22. What is simple interest on $180 at 6% for 2 years and 10 months?

    22.____

23. A painter added a pint of turpentine to every gallon of paint.
In 81 quarts of this mixture, how many gallons of paint were there?

    23.____

24. A man had $3.69 in change in his pocket. This consisted of an equal number of nickels, pennies, dimes, and quarters.
How many cents worth of nickels has he?

    24.____

25. *The constitution of any country, whether written or traditional, is the fundamental law of that country; that is, the highest law by which the country professes to be governed. If any law is made in violation of that fundamental law, it is of no force whatever, and is, to all intents and purposes, null and void. The history of different countries shows that legis-latures have sometimes attempted to pass such laws, but they have been set aside and declared inoperative by the law-interpreting branch of the government.*
Judging entirely by the preceding paragraph, which one of the following statement is TRUE?

    25.____

    A. Traditional laws are never included in a constitution.
    B. A constitution must be written to be legal.
    C. History shows that legislatures enforce laws that are in opposition to the constitu-tion.
    D. The law-interpreting branch of the government alone has the power to make laws.
    E. Laws made in violation of the constitution are not legal.

KEY (CORRECT ANSWERS)

1. 1800
2. 10
3. discipline
4. allegiance
5. nuisance

6. patrolling
7. separating
8. E
9. D
10. none

11. D
12. D
13. B
14. C
15. B

16. C
17. B
18. penitentiary
19. incredible
20. C

21. D
22. $30.60
23. 18
24. 45¢
25. E

TEST 2

DIRECTIONS: Each question or incomplete statement is followed by several suggested answers or completions. Select the one that BEST answers the question or completes the statement. *PRINT THE CORRECT ANSWER IN THE SPACE AT THE RIGHT.*

1. If 4 printing presses running together can complete a job in 12 hours, how long will it take 6 presses running together to do the same job?   1._____

2. Which one of the following answers can be applied to both BUS and STREETCAR but not to AUTOMOBILE?   2._____

   A. Carry people   B. Have chauffeurs
   C. Motor driven   D. Public conveyances
   E. Rubber-tired

3. LAMP-WICK is to OIL as MOTOR is to   3._____

   A. automobile   B. locomotive   C. mechanic
   D. gasoline   E. alcohol

4. LOCOMOTIVE is to SMOKESTACK as HOUSE is to   4._____

   A. living quarters   B. brick   C. furnace
   D. chimney   E. window

5. *That the Indian is taking a large part in administering the affairs of his own race is disclosed in a survey showing that approximately one-third of the employees of the Indian Bureau are Indians. These appointments were not made merely because the person applying was an Indian, but because he or she was found to be the best equipped person for the job. Officials at the Indian Bureau believe that the employment of Indians tends to make them more satisfied and proves an incentive to others of their race to fill responsible positions. The Indian brings to the service an understanding of his fellow men that few white people have.*   5._____
   The above paragraph states that the Indian is now taking a large part in administering the affairs of his own race because

   A. by nature he is best fitted to do this
   B. this is an incentive to others of his race
   C. he understands his people best and should, therefore, take part in administering their affairs even if he is not so competent as a white man
   D. by training he has been equipped to hold responsible positions
   E. approximately one-third of all the Indians are now in the government service

6. The postal clerk at the stamp window sold seven 3¢ stamps to every six 2¢ stamps. Altogether he sold 533 stamps. How many 3¢ stamps did he sell?   6._____

7. Art and Dave work together for 4 minutes on an assignment of 2316 pieces of mail; then Clem joins them.   7._____
   How long will it take the three of them to finish the lot if Art can sort at the rate of 57 pieces per minute, Dave at the rate of 48 per minute, and Clem at the rate of 53 per minute?

8. 2/3 of the first number equals 1/4 of the second number. This second number would be doubled by adding 24 to it. What is the FIRST number?   8._____

9. SEED is to PLANT as EGG is to

    A. food   B. nest   C. hatched
    D. chicken   E. healthful

9.____

10. *All debts contracted, and engagements entered into, shall be as valid against the United States, under this constitution, as under the Confederacy.*
What one word in the above sentence describes the condition which is lawfully sound and good?

10.____

11. Parcels and letters shall be examined as to their condition and then recorded.
What one word in the above sentence has the same meaning as *inspected*?

11.____

12. Who calls an election if a vacancy exists in the representation from any state?

    A. Governor   B. President   C. Congress
    D. Supreme Court   E. People

12.____

13. A VAGRANT is a

    A. land grant   B. vegetable   C. wanderer
    D. tradition   E. moron

13.____

14. AUTOMOBILE is to GARAGE as AIRSHIP is to

    A. balloon   B. pilot   C. hangar
    D. aviator   E. commander

14.____

15. WISCONSIN is to UNITED STATES as PART is to

    A. Ohio   B. whole   C. hand
    D. British Isles   E. separation

15.____

16. *The greatest wealth is health* means MOST NEARLY

    A. he who wants health wants everything
    B. a good wife and health are a man's best wealth
    C. he who is well has half won the battle
    D. health is the best wealth
    E. people with wealth can preserve their health

16.____

17. An AUTHENTIC statement is one which is

    A. false   B. true   C. formal
    D. genuine   E. likely

17.____

18. *In many foreign countries, the first one to register a trademark is considered to be the owner. Many American manufacturers who failed to register their trademarks abroad have found themselves in hot water because foreign trademark pirates have held them up for large sums of money in exchange for the stolen trademarks. As these pirates are in a position to exclude the goods of the real manufacturer from their country, the American manufacturer who happened to be asleep has to come to some agreement with them.*
Judging from the above paragraph, which one of the following statements is TRUE?

    A. A trademark registered in a foreign country is not protected.
    B. Foreign courts are partial to their own citizens.

18.____

C. American trademarks, when not registered in many foreign countries, may be claimed and registered there by residents as their own.

D. It is necessary for Americans to pay large sums of money to register their trademarks in foreign countries.

E. Trademarks registered in the United States are thereby protected all over the world.

19. A YIELDING body is one which   19.____

    A. resists   B. forces   C. gives
    D. is obstinate   E. crumbles

20. ESTEEM is to DESPISE as FRIENDS are to   20.____

    A. lovers   B. enemies   C. men
    D. acquaintances   E. people

21. *The right of citizens of the United States to vote shall not be denied or abridged by the*   21.____
United States or by any state on account of race, color, or previous condition of servi-
tude.
According to the above paragraph, it is TRUE that any

    A. colored person who has served as a slave may not vote
    B. person who has lived in the United States for 5 years cannot vote
    C. person who has come here from abroad can vote
    D. person who has lived in the United States for 5 years can vote
    E. citizen of the United States has the right to vote

22. The legislative part of our government is the   22.____

    A. supreme court   B. president   C. cabinet
    D. congress   E. people

23. ABIDE is to STAY as DEPART is to   23.____

    A. early   B. late   C. come   D. leave   E. hasten

24. *A national-origins clause added to our immigration laws would bring a heavy diminish-*   24.____
ment of immigration from Germany, Ireland, and the Scandinavian countries; but would
add greatly to the number of immigrants admitted from Britain, due to the numerical
rights of the original revolutionary inhabitants of this country, most of whom were British.
Judging from the above paragraph, which one of the following statements is TRUE?

    A. A national-origins clause would bring a heavy increase in the number of German and Irish immigrants admitted to the U.S.
    B. More British would be admitted under this clause because so many British inhabitants of this country took part in the revolutionary war.
    C. More British immigrants would be admitted because the number of British inhabitants in this country, originally, was greatest.
    D. Many Germans, Irish, and Scandinavians would be deported from the U.S.
    E. British people would be preferred to other races.

25. Which body makes the laws governing immigration?   25.____

    A. Supreme Court   B. Congress
    C. President   D. Senate
    E. Department of Labor

KEY (CORRECT ANSWERS)

1.	8 hrs.		11.	examined
2.	D		12.	A
3.	D		13.	C
4.	D		14.	C
5.	D		15.	B
6.	287		16.	D
7.	12		17.	B
8.	9		18.	C
9.	D		19.	C
10.	Valid		20.	B

21. E
22. D
23. D
24. C
25. B

TEST 3

DIRECTIONS: Each question or incomplete statement is followed by several suggested answers or completions. Select the one that BEST answers the question or completes the statement. *PRINT THE CORRECT ANSWER IN THE SPACE AT THE RIGHT.*

1. ABUNDANT is to SCARCE as CHEAP is to   1.____

   A. bargain   B. buy   C. costly
   D. disagreeable   E. value

2. A WEARY horse is one which is   2.____

   A. easily refreshed   B. jaded
   C. young   D. enthusiastic
   E. breathing heavily

3. A VIRTUOUS person is a   3.____

   A. waster   B. poor friend
   C. person with morals   D. profligate
   E. friendly person

4. *Economy is a great revenue* means MOST NEARLY   4.____

   A. ask thy purse what thou shouldst buy
   B. from saving comes having
   C. penny by penny laid up will be many
   D. he who eats and saves sets the table twice
   E. thrice lucky is he who can save

5. Who is the Speaker of the House of Representatives?   5.____

   A. Vice President
   B. Sergeant-at-arms
   C. President
   D. Representative elected for this purpose
   E. Secretary of State

6. WASHINGTON is to LINCOLN as FIRST is to   6.____

   A. last   B. president   C. sixteenth
   D. Roosevelt   E. republican

7. An UNUSUAL person is   7.____

   A. odd   B. friendly   C. common
   D. kind   E. loud

8. If the President nominates most of the government's important officials, which body con-   8.____
   firms the appointment?

   A. Senate   B. House of Representatives
   C. Supreme Court   D. Vice President
   E. People

9. PARENT is to COMMAND as CHILD is to   9.____

   A. obey   B. will   C. women
   D. achieve   E. love

10. *Safe is the man who owes nothing* means MOST NEARLY   10._____

    A. pay your debts and go to sleep
    B. he who pays his debts grows rich
    C. words pay no debts
    D. out of debt, out of danger
    E. the man who owes nothing need not fear lawsuits

11. A UNITED army is one which is   11._____

    A. attacked   B. disrupted   C. asunder
    D. joined   E. powerful

12. EYE is to HEAD as WINDOW is to   12._____

    A. ceiling   B. key   C. room
    D. door   E. wall

13. A man increased the speed of his car by 50%. After this increase, he was going 90 miles   13._____
per hour.
What was his speed before the increasethe

14. *The Texas law, putting a curb on oil production, was overwhelmingly passed by both*   14._____
houses of the legislature. The governor had threatened to use martial law to enforce a
shutdown of oil wells if the legislators took no action.
Judging entirely from the above paragraph, it is TRUE that

    A. martial law was used to shut down oil wells in Texas
    B. legislators refused to take action in curbing oil production
    C. the legislature passed a bill which could curb oil production
    D. the Governor threatened to use martial law in compelling the legislature to take
       action
    E. the legislature decided to use the militia to control oil production

15. *It is evident that the fitness of the Philippine people to maintain a popular independent*   15._____
government will be closely dependent upon the education of the masses. It is important
that a clear understanding of the educational work in the Philippines should be reached
as there is much popular misapprehension on the subject. Before the Spanish-American
war, the only history ever taught was that of Spain, and that under censorship; the history
of other countries was a closed volume to the Filipino. The only educational advantage
attainable by the common people was that afforded by the primary schools, which was a
wretchedly inadequate provision.
Judging entirely from the above paragraph, which one of the following statements is
TRUE?
The fitness of the Philippine people to maintain an independent government is dependent upon

    A. the education of the people
    B. history being censored before it is taught in the schools
    C. popular support of the government
    D. their knowledge of the world's history
    E. their freedom from Spain

16. To ABANDON is to   16._____

    A. forsake   B. cherish   C. keep
    D. recall   E. forget

17. CLOTHES are to MAN as HAIR is to   17._____

    A. coat   B. dog   C. comb   D. pretty   E. cut

18. DIAMOND is to RARE as IRON is to   18._____

    A. silver   B. ore   C. common
    D. tin   E. valuable

19. *Gilbert K. Chesterton, in the course of his weekly attacks on the foibles of the day, has*   19._____
been turning his attention to the familiar assertion that 'in every age people have
thought their own age prosaic and only the past poetical'–in other words, that, while the
glamour of antiquity adds interest and prestige to the past, the present always seems
dull to its people, who take a morose pleasure in comparing it unfavorably with the 'good
old times.'
Judging entirely by the above paragraph, which one of the following statements is
TRUE?
Mr. Chesterton attacks and denies the assertion that

    A. people think the past is poetical and interesting
    B. people think their own time is commonplace and uninteresting
    C. we compare our times favorably with *the good old times*
    D. the past holds no interest for us
    E. the glamour of age is not adding prestige to our age

20. *One of the best and most cheerful signs of American interest in matters other than the*   20._____
purely material is the rapid increase of commercial buildings which are artistic. That a
railway company should introduce decorative and ceramic art into its power house, for
example, is surprising and cannot result in any immediate cash profit. Yet that is what
one company has done. Located in the heart of a dingy and deserted slum district in one
of our large cities, there is a great building of the finest white stone, designed by one of
the best architects in America. It is simple, neither plain nor severe, but dignified and
beautiful. It is already exerting an uplifting and beneficient effect upon the neighborhood.
Judging entirely by the statements given above, select the ONLY one of the following
statements that corresponds exactly with the paragraph.

    A. All beautiful buildings are simple in design.
    B. To beautify a power house cannot result in any immediate cash return.
    C. Americans are interested only in purely material things.
    D. Beautiful buildings are always placed in slum districts to uplift and benefit the
        neighborhood.
    E. There would be no dingy slum districts if Americans were interested in things not
        only purely material.

21. To mislead is to DESEEV.   21._____
The word in capitals is misspelled. Write it correctly at the right.

22. A small PARTIKUL remained.   22.___
    The word in capitals is misspelled. Write it correctly at the right.

23. Mules are known to be STUBURN.   23.___
    The word in capitals is misspelled. Write it correctly at the right.

24. 152 is 19% of a number.   24.___
    What is 7% of that same number.

25. If a man paid $24 for pigeons, and 12 pigeons died, and then he sold 3/7 of the rest at   25.___
    cost for $9, how many pigeons did he buy?

KEY (CORRECT ANSWERS)

1.	C	11.	D
2.	B	12.	C
3.	C	13.	60
4.	B	14.	C
5.	D	15.	A
6.	C	16.	A
7.	A	17.	B
8.	A	18.	C
9.	A	19.	B
10.	D	20.	B

21. deceive
22. particle
23. stubborn
24. 56
25. 96

VERBAL ABILITIES TEST

DIRECTIONS AND SAMPLE QUESTIONS

Study the sample questions carefully. Each question has four suggested answers. Decide which one is the best answer. Find the question number on the Sample Answer Sheet. Show your answer to the question by darkening completely the space corresponding to the letter that is the same as the letter of your answer. Keep your mark within the space. If you have to erase a mark, be sure to erase it completely. Mark only one answer for each question. Do NOT mark space E for any question.

SAMPLE VERBAL QUESTIONS

I. *Previous* means most nearly

    A. abandoned   C. timely
    B. former   D. younger

II. *(Reading)* "Just as the procedure of a collection department must be clear cut and definite, the steps being taken with the sureness of a skilled chess player, so the various paragraphs of a collection letter must show clear organization, giving evidence of a mind that, from the beginning, has had a specific end in view."
The quotation best supports the statement that a collection letter should always

    A. show a spirit of sportsmanship
    B. be divided into several paragraphs
    C. be brief, but courteous
    D. be carefully planned

III. Decide which sentence is preferable with respect to grammar and usage suitable for a formal letter or report.

    A. They do not ordinarily present these kind of reports in detail like this.
    B. A report of this kind is not hardly ever given in such detail as this one.
    C. This report is more detailed than what such reports ordinarily are.
    D. A report of this kind is not ordinarily presented in as much detail as this one is.

IV. Find the correct spelling of the word and darken the proper answer space. If no suggested spelling is correct, darken space D.

    A. athalete   C. athlete
    B. athelete   D. none of these

V. SPEEDOMETER is related to POINTER as WATCH is related to

    A. case   C. dial
    B. hands   D. numerals

EXAMINATION SECTION
TEST 1

Read each question carefully. Select the best answer and darken the proper space on the answer sheet.

1. *Flexible* means most nearly

   A. breakable
   B. flammable
   C. pliable
   D. weak

2. *Option* means most nearly

   A. use
   B. choice
   C. value
   D. blame

3. To *verify* means most nearly to

   A. examine
   B. explain
   C. confirm
   D. guarantee

4. *Indolent* means most nearly

   A. moderate
   B. hopeless
   C. selfish
   D. lazy

5. *Respiration* means most nearly

   A. recovery
   B. breathing
   C. pulsation
   D. sweating

6. PLUMBER is related to WRENCH as PAINTER is related to

   A. brush
   B. pipe
   C. shop
   D. hammer

7. LETTER is related to MESSAGE as PACKAGE is related to

   A. sender
   B. merchandise
   C. insurance
   D. business

8. FOOD is related to HUNGER as SLEEP is related to

   A. night
   B. dream
   C. weariness
   D. rest

9. KEY is related to TYPEWRITER as DIAL is related to

   A. sun
   B. number
   C. circle
   D. telephone

Grammar

10. A. I think that they will promote whoever has the best record.
     B. The firm would have liked to have promoted all employees with good records.
     C. Such of them that have the best records have excellent prospects of promotion.
     D. I feel sure they will give the promotion to whomever has the best record.

11. A. The receptionist must answer courteously the questions of all them callers.
    B. The receptionist must answer courteously the questions what are asked by the callers.
    C. There would have been no trouble if the receptionist had have always answered courteously.
    D. The receptionist should answer courteously the questions of all callers.

Spelling

12. A. collapsible   C. collapseble
    B. collapseble   D. none of these

13. A. ambigeuous   C. ambiguous
    B. ambigeous   D. none of these

14. A. predesessor   C. predecesser
    B. predecesar   D. none of these

15. A. sanctioned   C. sanctionned
    B. sancktioned   D. none of these

Reading

16. "The secretarial profession is a very old one and has increased in importance with the passage of time. In modern times, the vast expansion of business and industry has greatly increased the need and opportunities for secretaries, and for the first time in history their number has become large."
    The quotation best supports the statement that the secretarial profession

    A. is older than business and industry
    B. did not exist in ancient times
    C. has greatly increased in size
    D. demands higher training than it did formerly

17. "Civilization started to move ahead more rapidly when man freed himself of the shackles that restricted his search for the truth."
    The quotation best supports the statement that the progress of civilization

    A. came as a result of man's dislike for obstacles
    B. did not begin until restrictions on learning were removed
    C. has been aided by man's efforts to find
    D. the truth is based on continually increasing efforts

18. *Vigilant* means most nearly

    A. sensible   C. suspicious
    B. watchful   D. restless

19. *Incidental* means most nearly

    A. independent   C. infrequent
    B. needless   D. casual

20. *Conciliatory* means most nearly

    A. pacific
    B. contentious
    C. obligatory
    D. offensive

21. *Altercation* means most nearly

    A. defeat
    B. concurrence
    C. controversy
    D. vexation

22. *Irresolute* means most nearly

    A. wavering
    B. insubordinate
    C. impudent
    D. unobservant

23. DARKNESS is related to SUNLIGHT as STILLNESS is related to

    A. quiet
    B. moonlight
    C. sound
    D. dark

24. DESIGNED is related to INTENTION as ACCIDENTAL is related to

    A. purpose
    B. caution
    C. damage
    D. chance

25. ERROR is related to PRACTICE as SOUND is related to

    A. deafness
    B. noise
    C. muffler
    D. horn

26. RESEARCH is related to FINDINGS as TRAINING is related to

    A. skill
    B. tests
    C. supervision
    D. teaching

27. A   If properly addressed, the letter will reach my mother and I.
    B. The letter had been addressed to myself and my mother,
    C. I believe the letter was addressed to either my mother or I.
    D. My mother's name, as well as mine, was on the letter.

28. A. The supervisor reprimanded the typist, whom she believed had made careless errors.
    B. The typist would have corrected the errors had she of known that the supervisor would see the report.
    C. The errors in the typed report were so numerous that they could hardly beoverlooked.
    D. Many errors were found in the report which she typed and could not disregard them.

29. A. minieture
    B. minneature
    C. mineature
    D. none of these

30. A. extemporaneous
    B. extempuraneus
    C. extemporaneous
    D. none of these

31. A. problemmatical
    B. problematical
    C. problematicle
    D. none of these

32.   A. descendant   C. desendant
      B. decendant   D. none of these

33. "The likelihood of America's exhausting her natural resources seems to be growing less. All kinds of waste are being reworked and new uses are constantly being found for almost everything. We are getting more use out of our goods and are making many new byproducts out of what was formerly thrown away."
The quotation best supports the statement that we seem to be in less danger of exhausting our resources because

    A. economy is found to lie in the use of substitutes
    B. more service is obtained from a given amount of material
    C. we are allowing time for nature to restore them
    D. supply and demand are better controlled

34. "Memos should be clear, concise, and brief. Omit all unnecessary words. The parts of speech most often used in memos are nouns, verbs, adjectives, and adverbs. If possible, do without pronouns, prepositions, articles and copulative verbs. Use simple sentences, rather than complex or compound ones."
The quotation best supports the statement that in writing memos one should always use

    A. common and simple words
    B. only nouns, verbs, adjectives, and adverbs
    C. incomplete sentences
    D. only the words essential to the meaning.

35. To *counteract* means most nearly to

    A. undermine   C. preserve
    B. censure   D. neutralize

36. *Deferred* means most nearly

    A. reversed   C. considered
    B. delayed   D. forbidden

37. *Feasible* means most nearly

    A. capable   C. practicable
    B. justifiable   D. beneficial

38. To *encounter* means most nearly to

    A. meet   C. overcome
    B. recall   D. retreat

39. *Innate* means most nearly

    A. eternal   C. native
    B. well-developed   D. prospective

40. STUDENT is related to TEACHER as DISCIPLE is related to

    A. follower   C. principal
    B. master   D. pupil

41. LECTURE is related to AUDITORIUM as EXPERIMENT is related to

    A. scientist   C. laboratory
    B. chemistry   D. discovery

42. BODY is related to FOOD as ENGINE is related to

    A. wheels   C. motion
    B. fuel   D. smoke

43. SCHOOL is related to EDUCATION as THEATER is related to

    A. management   C. recreation
    B. stage   D. preparation

44. A. Most all these statements have been supported by persons who are reliable and can be depended upon.
    B. The persons which have guaranteed these statements are reliable.
    C. Reliable persons guarantee the facts with regards to the truth of these statements.
    D. These statements can be depended on, for their truth has been guaranteed by reliable persons.

45. A. The success of the book pleased both his publisher and he.
    B. Both his publisher and he was pleased with the success of the book.
    C. Neither he or his publisher was disappointed with the success of the book.
    D. His publisher was as pleased as he with the success of the book

46. A. extercate   C. extricate
    B. extracate   D. none of these

47. A. hereditory   C. hereditairy
    B. hereditary   D. none of these

48. A. auspiceous   C. auspicious
    B. auspiseous   D. none of these

49. A. sequance   C. sequense
    B. sequence   D. none of these

50. "The prevention of accidents makes it necessary not only that safety devices be used to guard exposed machinery but also that mechanics be instructed in safety rules which they must follow for their own protection, and that the lighting in the plant be adequate."
The quotation best supports the statement that industrial accidents

    A. may be due to ignorance
    B. are always avoidable
    C. usually result from inadequate machinery
    D. cannot be entirely overcome

51. "The English language is peculiarly rich in synonyms, and there is scarcely a language spoken among men that has not some representative in English speech. The spirit of the Anglo-Saxon race has subjugated these various elements to one idiom, making not a patchwork, but a composite language."
The quotation best supports the statement that the English language

A. has few idiomatic expressions
B. is difficult to translate
C. is used universally
D. has absorbed words from other languages

52. To *acquiesce* means most nearly to

A. assent
B. acquire
C. complete
D. participate

53. *Unanimity* means most nearly

A. emphasis
B. namelessness
C. harmony
D. impartiality

54. *Precedent* means most nearly

A. example
B. theory
C. law
D. conformity

55. *Versatile* means most nearly

A. broad-minded
B. well-known
C. up-to-date
D. many-sided

56. *Authentic* means most nearly

A. detailed
B. reliable
C. valuable
D. practical

57. BIOGRAPHY is related to FACT as NOVEL is related to

A. fiction
B. literature
C. narration
D. book

58. COPY is related to CARBON PAPER as MOTION PICTURE is related to

A. theater
B. film
C. duplicate
D. television

59. EFFICIENCY is related to REWARD as CARELESSNESS is related to

A. improvement
B. disobedience
C. reprimand
D. repetition

60. ABUNDANT is related to CHEAP as SCARCE is related to

A. ample
B. costly
C. inexpensive
D. unobtainable

61. A Brown's & Company employees have recently received increases in salary.
B. Brown & Company recently increased the salaries of all its employees.
C. Recently, Brown & Company has increased their employees' salaries.
D. Brown & Company have recently increased the salaries of all its employees

62. A   In reviewing the typists' work reports, the job analyst found records of unusual typing speeds.
     B. It says in the job analyst's report that some employees type with great speed.
     C. The job analyst found that, in reviewing the typists' work reports, that some unusual typing speeds had been made.
     D. In the reports of typists' speeds, the job analyst found some records that are kind of unusual.

63. A. obliterate   C. obbliterate
     B. oblitterat   D. none of these

64. A. diagnoesis   C. diagnosis
     B. diagnossis   D. none of these

65. A. contenance   C. knowledge
     B. countenance   D. none of these

66. A. conceivably   C. conceiveably
     B. concieveably   D. none of these

67. "Through advertising, manufacturers exercise a high degree of control over consumers' desires. However, the manufacturer assumes enormous risks in attempting to predict what consumers will want and in producing goods in quantity and distributing them in advance of final selection by the consumers."
     The quotation best supports the statement that manufacturers

     A. can eliminate the risk of overproduction by advertising
     B. distribute goods directly to the consumers
     C. must depend upon the final consumers for the success of their undertakings
     D. can predict with great accuracy the success of any product they put on the market

68. "In the relations of man to nature, the procuring of food and shelter is fundamental. With the migration of man to various climates, ever new adjustments to the food supply and to the climate became necessary."
     The quotation best supports the statement that the means by which man supplies his material needs are

     A. accidental
     B. varied
     C. limited
     D. inadequate

69. *Strident* means most nearly

     A. swaggering   C. angry
     B. domineering   D. harsh

70. To *confine* means most nearly to

     A. hide   C. eliminate
     B. restrict   D. punish

71. To *accentuate* means most nearly to

     A. modify   C. sustain
     B. hasten   D. intensify

72. *Banal* means most nearly

    A. commonplace   C. tranquil
    B. forceful   D. indifferent

73. *Incorrigible* means most nearly

    A. intolerable   C. irreformable
    B. retarded   D. brazen

74. POLICEMAN is related to ORDER as DOCTOR is related to

    A. physician   C. sickness
    B. hospital   D. health

75. ARTIST is related to EASEL as WEAVER is related to

    A. loom   C. threads
    B. cloth   D. spinner

76. CROWD is related to PERSONS as FLEET is related to

    A. expedition   C. navy
    B. officers   D. ships

77. CALENDAR is related to DATE as MAP is related to

    A. geography   C. mileage
    B. trip   D. vacation

78.   A   Since the report lacked the needed information, it was of no use to him.
    B.   This report was useless to him because there were no needed information in it.
    C.   Since the report did not contain the needed information, it was not real useful to him.
    D.   Being that the report lacked the needed information, he could not use it.

79.   A   The company had hardly declared the dividend till the notices were prepared for mailing.
    B.   They had no sooner declared the dividend when they sent the notices to the stockholders.
    C.   No sooner had the dividend been declared than the notices were prepared for mailing.
    D.   Scarcely had the dividend been declared than the notices were sent out.

80.   A. competition   C. competetion
    B. competition   D. none of these

81.   A. occassion   C. ocassion
    B. occasion   D. none of these

82.   A. knowlege   C. knowledge
    B. knolledge   D. none of these

83.   A. deliborate   C. delibrate
    B. deliberate   D. none of these

84. "What constitutes skill in any line of work is not always easy to determine; economy of time must be carefully distinguished from economy of energy, as the quickest method may require the greatest expenditure of muscular effort, and may not be essential or at all desirable."
The quotation best supports the statement that

   A. the most efficiently executed task is not always the one done in the shortest time
   B. energy and time cannot both be conserved in performing a single task
   C. a task is well done when it is performed in the shortest time
   D. skill in performing a task should not be acquired at the expense of time

85. "It is difficult to distinguish between bookkeeping and accounting. In attempts to do so, bookkeeping is called the art, and accounting the science, of recording business transactions. Bookkeeping gives the history of the business in a systematic manner; and accounting classifies, analyzes, and interprets the facts thus recorded."
The quotation best supports the statement that

   A. accounting is less systematic than bookkeeping
   B. accounting and bookkeeping are closely related
   C. bookkeeping and accounting cannot be distinguished from one another
   D. bookkeeping has been superseded by accounting

KEY (CORRECT ANSWERS)

1. C	21. C	41. C	61. B	81. B
2. B	22. A	42. B	62. A	82. C
3. C	23. C	43. C	63. A	83. B
4. D	24. D	44. D	64. C	84. A
5. B	25. C	45. D	65. B	85. B
6. A	26. A	46. C	66. A	
7. B	27. D	47. B	67. C	
8. C	28. C	48. C	68. B	
9. D	29. D	49. B	69. D	
10. A	30. A	50. A	70. B	
11. D	31. B	51. D	71. D	
12. A	32. A	52. A	72. A	
13. C	33. B	53. C	73. C	
14. D	34. D	54. A	74. D	
15. A	35. D	55. D	75. A	
16. C	36. B	56. B	76. D	
17. C	37. C	57. A	77. C	
18. B	38. A	58. B	78. A	
19. D	39. C	59. C	79. C	
20. A	40. B	60. B	80. B	

TEST 2

Read each question carefully. Select the best answer and blacken the proper space on the answer sheet.

1. *Option* means most nearly

   A. use
   B. choice
   C. value
   D. blame
   E. mistake

2. *Irresolute* means most nearly

   A. wavering
   B. insubordinate
   C. impudent
   D. determined
   E. unobservant

3. *Flexible* means most nearly

   A. breakable
   B. inflammable
   C. pliable
   D. weak
   E. impervious

4. To *counteract* means most nearly to

   A. undermine
   B. censure
   C. preserve
   D. sustain
   E. neutralize

5. To *verify* means most nearly to

   A. justify
   B. explain
   C. confirm
   D. guarantee
   E. examine

6. *Indolent* means most nearly

   A. moderate
   B. relentless
   C. selfish
   D. lazy
   E. hopeless

7. To say that an action is *deferred* means most nearly that it is

   A. delayed
   B. reversed
   C. considered
   D. forbidden
   E. followed

8. To *encounter* means most nearly to

   A. meet
   B. recall
   C. overcome
   D. weaken
   E. retreat

9. *Feasible* means most nearly

   A. capable
   B. practicable
   C. justifiable
   D. beneficial
   E. reliable

10. *Respiration* means most nearly

   A. dehydration
   B. breathing
   C. pulsation
   D. sweating
   E. recovery

11. *Vigilant* means most nearly

   A. sensible
   B. ambitious
   C. watchful
   D. suspicious
   E. restless

12. To say that an action is taken *before the proper time* means most nearly that it is taken

   A. prematurely
   B. furtively
   C. temporarily
   D. punctually
   E. presently

13. *Innate* means most nearly

   A. eternal
   B. learned
   C. native
   D. prospective
   E. well-developed

14. *Precedent* means most nearly

   A. duplicate
   B. theory
   C. law
   D. conformity
   E. example

15. To say that the flow of work into an office is *incessant* means most nearly that it is

   A. more than can be handled
   B. uninterrupted
   C. scanty
   D. decreasing in volume
   E. orderly

16. *Unanimity* means most nearly

   A. emphasis
   B. namelessness
   C. disagreement
   D. harmony
   E. impartiality

17. *Incidental* means most nearly

   A. independent
   B. needless
   C. infrequent
   D. necessary
   E. casual

18. *Versatile* means most nearly

   A. broad-minded
   B. well-Known
   C. old-fashioned
   D. many-sided
   E. up-to-date

19. *Conciliatory* means most nearly

   A. pacific
   B. contentious
   C. disorderly

   D. obligatory
   E. offensive

20. *Altercation* means most nearly

   A. defeat
   B. concurrence
   C. controversy

   D. consensus
   E. vexation

21. *(Reading)* "The secretarial profession is a very old one and has increased in importance with the passage of time. In modern times, the vast expansion of business and industry has greatly increased the need and opportunities for secretaries, and for the first time in history their number has become large."

   The quotation best supports the statement that the secretarial profession

   A. is older than business and industry
   B. did not exist in ancient times
   C. has greatly increased in size
   D. demands higher training than it did formerly
   E. has always had many members

22. *(Reading)* "The modern system of production unites various kinds of workers into a well-organized body in which each has a definite place."
   The quotation best supports the statement that the modern system of production

   A. increases production
   B. trains workers
   C. simplifies tasks
   D. combines and places workers
   E. combines the various plants

23. *(Reading)* "The prevention of accidents makes it necessary not only that safety devices be used to guard exposed machinery but also that mechanics be instructed in safety rules which they must follow for their own protection, and that the lighting in the plant be adequate."

   The quotation best supports the statement that industrial accidents

   A. may be due to ignorance
   B. are always avoidable
   C. usually result from inadequate machinery
   D. cannot be entirely overcome
   E. result in damage to machinery

24. *(Reading)* "It is wise to choose a duplicating machine that will do the work required with the greatest efficiency and at the least cost. Users with a large volume of business need speedy machines that cost little to operate and are well made."

   The quotation best supports the statement that

A. most users of duplicating machines prefer low operating cost to efficiency
B. a well-built machine will outlast a cheap one
C. a duplicating machine is not efficient unless it is sturdy
D. a duplicating machine should be both efficient and economical
E. in duplicating machines speed is more usual than low operating cost

25. *(Reading)* "The likelihood of America's exhausting her natural resources seems to be growing less. All kinds of waste are being reworked and new uses are constantly being found for almost everything. We are getting more use out of our goods and are making many new byproducts out of what was formerly thrown away."

The quotation best supports the statement that we seem to be in less danger of exhausting our resources because

A. economy is found to lie in the use of substitutes
B. more service is obtained from a given amount of material
C. more raw materials are being produced
D. supply and demand are better controlled
E. we are allowing time for nature to restore them

26. *(Reading)* "Probably few people realize, as they drive on a concrete road, that steel is used to keep the surface flat and even, in spite of the weight of busses and trucks. Steel bars, deeply imbedded in the concrete, provide sinews to take the stresses so that they cannot crack the slab or make it wavy."

The quotation best supports the statement that a concrete road

A. is expensive to build
B. usually cracks under heavy weights
C. looks like any other road
D. is used exclusively for heavy traffic
E. is reinforced with other material

27. *(Reading)* "Through advertising, manufacturers exercise a high degree of control over consumers' desires. However, the manufac-turer assumes enormous risks in attempting to predict what consumers will want and in producing goods in quantity and distributing them in advance of final selection by the consumers."

The quotation best supports the statement that manufacturers

A. can eliminate the risk of overproduction by advertising
B. completely control buyers' needs and desires
C. must depend upon the final consumers for the success of their undertakings
D. distribute goods directly to the consumers
E. can predict with great accuracy the success of any product they put on the market

28. *(Reading)* "Success in shorthand, like success in any other study, depends upon the interest the student takes in it. In writing shorthand it is not sufficient to know how to write a word correctly; one must also be able to write it quickly."

The quotation best supports the statement that

A. one must be able to read shorthand as well as to write it
B. shorthand requires much study
C. if a student can write correctly, he can also write quickly
D. proficiency in shorthand requires both speed and accuracy
E. interest in shorthand makes study unnecessary

29. *(Reading)* "The countries in the Western Hemisphere were settled by people who were ready each day for new adventure. The peoples of North and South America have retained, in addition to expectant and forwardlooking attitudes, the ability and the willingness that they have often shown in the past to adapt themselves to new conditions."

The quotation best supports the statement that the peoples in the Western Hemisphere

A. no longer have fresh adventures daily
B. are capable of making changes as new situations arise
C. are no more forward-looking than the peoples of other regions
D. tend to resist regulations
E. differ considerably among themselves

30. *(Reading)* "Civilization started to move ahead more rapidly when man freed himself of the shackles that restricted his search for the truth."
The quotation best supports the statement that the progress of civilization

A. came as a result of man's dislike for obstacles
B. did not begin until restrictions on learning were removed
C. has been aided by man's efforts to find the truth
D. is based on continually increasing efforts
E. continues at a constantly increasing rate

31. *(Reading)* "It is difficult to distinguish between bookkeeping and accounting. In attempts to do so, bookkeeping is called the art, and accounting the science, of recording business transactions. Bookkeeping gives the history of the business in a systematic manner, and accounting classifies, analyzes, and interprets the facts thus recorded."

The quotation best supports the statement that

A. accounting is less systematic than bookkeeping
B. accounting and bookkeeping are closely related
C. bookkeeping and accounting cannot be distinguished from one another
D. bookkeeping has been superseded by accounting
E. the facts recorded by bookkeeping may be interpreted in many ways

32. *(Reading)* "Some specialists are willing to give their services to the Government entirely free of charge; some feel that a nominal salary, such as will cover traveling expenses, is sufficient for a position that is recognized as being somewhat honorary in nature; many other specialists value their time so highly that they will not devote any of it to public service that does not repay them at a rate commensurate with the fees that they can obtain from a good private clientele."

The quotation best supports the statement that the use of specialists by the Government

A. is rare because of the high cost of securing such persons
B. may be influenced by the willingness of specialists to serve
C. enables them to secure higher salaries in private fields
D. has become increasingly common during the past few years
E. always conflicts with private demands for their services

33. *(Reading)* "The leader of an industrial enterprise has two principal functions. He must manufacture and distribute a product at a profit, and he must keep individuals and groups of individuals working effectively together."

    The quotation best supports the statement that an industrial leader should be able to

    A. increase the distribution of his plant's product
    B. introduce large-scale production methods
    C. coordinate the activities of his employees
    D. profit by the experience of other leaders
    E. expand the business rapidly

34. *(Reading)* "The coloration of textile fabrics composed of cotton and wool generally requires two processes, as the process used in dyeing wool is seldom capable of fixing the color upon cotton. The usual method is to immerse the fabric in the requisite baths to dye the wool and then to treat the partially dyed material in the manner found suitable for cotton."
    The quotation best supports the statement that the dyeing of textile fabrics composed of cotton and wool

    A. is less complicated than the dyeing of wool alone
    B. is more successful when the material contains more cotton than wool
    C. is not satisfactory when solid colors are desired
    D. is restricted to two colors for any one fabric
    E. is usually based upon the methods required for dyeing the different materials

35. *(Reading)* "The fact must not be overlooked that only about one-half of the international trade of the world crosses the oceans. The other half is merely exchanges of merchandise between countries lying alongside each other or at least within the same continent."

    The quotation best supports the statement that

    A. the most important part of any country's trade is transoceanic
    B. domestic trade is insignificant when compared with foreign trade
    C. the exchange of goods between neighboring countries is not considered international trade
    D. foreign commerce is not necessarily carried on by water
    E. about one-half of the trade of the world is international

36. *(Reading)* "In the relations of man to nature, the procuring of food and shelter is fundamental. With the migration of man to various climates, ever new adjustments to the food supply and to the climate became necessary."

    The quotation best supports the statement that the means by which man supplies his material needs are

A. accidental   D. uniform
B. varied   E. inadequate
C. limited

37. *(Reading)* "Every language has its peculiar word associations that have no basis in logic and cannot therefore be reasoned about. These idiomatic expressions are ordinarily acquired only by much reading and conversation although questions about such matters may sometimes be answered by the dictionary. Dictionaries large enough to include quota-tions from standard authors are especially serviceable in determining questions of idiom."

The quotation best supports the statement that idiomatic expressions

     A. give rise to meaningless arguments because they have no logical basis
     B. are widely used by recognized authors.
     C. are explained in most dictionaries
     D. are more common in some languages than in others
     E. are best learned by observation of the language as actually used

38. *(Reading)* "Individual differences in mental traits assume importance in fitting workers to jobs because such personal characteristics are persistent and are relatively little influenced by training and experience."

The quotation best supports the statement that training and experience

     A. are limited in their effectiveness in fitting workers to jobs
     B. do not increase a worker's fitness for a job
     C. have no effect upon a person's mental traits
     D. have relatively little effect upon the individual's chances for success
     E. should be based on the mental traits of an individual

39. *(Reading)* "The telegraph networks of the country now constitute wonderfully operated institutions, affording for ordinary use of modern, business an important means of communication. The transmission of messages by electricity has reached the goal for which the postal service has long been striving, namely, the elimination of distance as an effective barrier of communication."

The quotation best supports the statement that

     A. a new standard of communication has been attained
     B. in the telegraph service, messages seldom go astray
     C. it is the distance between the parties which creates the need for communication
     D. modern business relies more upon the telegraph than upon the mails
     E. the telegraph is a form of postal service

40. *(Reading)* "The competition of buyers tends to keep prices up, the competition of sellers to send them down. Normally the pressure of competition among sellers is stronger than that among buyers since the seller has his article to sell and must get rid of it, whereas the buyer is not committed to anything."

The quotation best supports the statement that low prices are caused by

A. buyer competition
B. competition of buyers with sellers fluctuations in demand
C. greater competition among sellers than among buyers
D. more sellers than buyers

In each question from 41 through 60, find the CORRECT spelling of the word, and blacken the proper space on your answer sheet. Sometimes there is no correct spelling; if none of the suggested spellings is correct, blacken space D on your answer sheet.

41. A. compitition
    B. competition
    C. competetion
    D. none of these

42. A. diagnoesis
    B. diagnossis
    C. diagnosis
    D. none of these

43. A. contenance
    B. countenance
    C. countinance
    D. none of these

44. A. deliborate
    B. deliberate
    C. delibrate
    D. none of these

45. A. knowlege
    B. knolledge
    C. knowledge
    D. none of these

46. A. occassion
    B. occasion
    C. ocassion
    D. none of these

47. A. sanctioned
    B. sancktioned
    C. sanctionned
    D. none of these

48. A. predesessor
    B. predecesar
    C. predecesser
    D. none of these

49. A. problemmatical
    B. problematical
    C. problematicle
    D. none of these

50. A. descendant
    B. decendant
    C. desendant
    D. none of these

51. A. collapsible
    B. collapseable
    C. collapseble
    D. none of these

52. A. sequance
    B. sequence
    C. sequense
    D. none of these

53. A. oblitorate
    B. oblitterat
    C. obbliterate
    D. none of these

54. A. ambigeuous
    B. ambigeous
    C. ambiguous
    D. none of these

55. A. minieture
    B. minneature
    C. mineature
    D. none of these

56. A. extemporaneous
    B. extempuraneus
    C. extemperaneous
    D. none of these

57.   A. hereditory   C. hereditairy
        B. hereditary   D. none of these

58.   A. conceivably   C. conceiveably
        B. concieveably   D. none of these

59.   A. extercate   C. extricate
        B. extracate   D. none of these

60.   A. auspiceous   C. auspicious
        B. auspiseous   D. none of these

Select the sentence that is preferable with respect to grammar and usage such as would be suitable in a formal letter or report. Then blacken the proper space on the answer sheet.

61.   A   The receptionist must answer courteously the questions of all them callers.
       B. The questions of all callers had ought to be answered courteously.
       C. The receptionist must answer courteously the questions what are asked by the callers.
       D. There would have been no trouble if the receptionist had have always answered courteously.
       E. The receptionist should answer courteously the questions of all callers.

62.   A   I had to learn a great number of rules, causing me to dislike the course.
       B. I disliked that study because it required the learning of numerous rules.
       C. I disliked that course very much, caused by the numerous rules I had to memorize.
       D. The cause of my dislike was on account of the numerous rules I had to learn in that course.
       E. The reason I disliked this study was because there were numerous rules that had to be learned.

63.   A   If properly addressed, the letter will reach my mother and I.
       B. The letter had been addressed to myself and mother.
       C. I believe the letter was addressed to either my mother or I.
       D. My mother's name, as well as mine, was on the letter.
       E. If properly addressed, the letter it will reach either my mother or me.

64.   A   A knowledge of commercial subjects and a mastery of English are essential if one wishes to be a good secretary.
       B. Two things necessary to a good secretary are that she should speak good English and to know commercial subjects.
       C. One cannot be a good secretary without she knows commercial subjects and English grammar.
       D. Having had good training in commercial subjects, the rules of English grammar should also be followed.
       E. A secretary seldom or ever succeeds without training in English as well as in commercial subjects.

65. A   He suspicions that the service is not so satisfactory as it should be.
    B.   He believes that we should try and find whether the service is satisfactory.
    C.   He raises the objection that the way which the service is given is not satisfactory.
    D.   He believes that the quality of our services are poor.
    E.   He believes that the service that we are giving is unsatisfactory.

66. A   Most all these statements have been supported by persons who are reliable and can be depended upon.
    B.   The persons which have guaranteed these statements are reliable.
    C.   Reliable persons guarantee the facts with regards to the truth of these statements.
    D.   These statements can be depended on, for their truth has been guaranteed by reliable persons.
    E.   Persons as reliable as what these are can be depended upon to make accurate statements.

67. A   Brown's & Company's employees have all been given increases in salary.
    B.   Brown & Company recently increased the salaries of all its employees.
    C.   Recently Brown & Company has in-creased their employees' salaries.
    D.   Brown's & Company employees have recently received increases in salary.
    E.   Brown & Company have recently increased the salaries of all its employees.

68. A.   The personnel office has charge of employment, dismissals, and employee's welfare.
    B.   Employment, together with dismissals and employees' welfare, are handled by the personnel department.
    C.   The personnel office takes charge of employment, dismissals, and etc.
    D.   The personnel office hires and dismisses employees, and their welfare is also its responsibility.
    E.   The personnel office is responsible for the employment, dismissal, and welfare of employees.

69. A.   This kind of pen is some better than that kind.
    B.   I prefer having these pens than any other.
    C.   This kind of pen is the most satisfactory for my use.
    D.   In comparison with that kind of pen, this kind is more preferable.
    E.   If I were to select between them all, I should pick this pen.

70. A.   He could not make use of the report, as it was lacking of the needed information.
    B.   This report was useless to him because there were no needed information in it.
    C.   Since the report lacked the needed information, it was of no use to him.
    D.   Being that the report lacked the needed information, he could not use it.
    E.   Since the report did not contain the needed information, it was not real useful to him.

71. A.   The paper we use for this purpose must be light, glossy, and stand hard usage as well.
    B.   Only a light and a glossy, but durable, paper must be used for this purpose.
    C.   For this purpose, we want a paper that is light, glossy, but that will stand hard wear.
    D.   For this purpose, paper that is light, glossy, and durable is essential.
    E.   Light and glossy paper, as well as standing hard usage, is necessary for this purpose.

72. A The company had hardly declared the dividend till the notices were prepared for mailing.
    B. They had no sooner declared the dividend when they sent the notices to the stockholders.
    C. No sooner had the dividend been declared than the notices were prepared for mailing.
    D. Scarcely had the dividend been declared than the notices were sent out.
    E. The dividend had not scarcely been declared when the notices were ready for mailing.

73. A Of all the employees, he spends the most time at the office.
    B. He spends more time at the office than that of his employees.
    C. His working hours are longer or at least equal to those of the other employees.
    D. He devotes as much, if not more, time to his work than the rest of the employees.
    E. He works the longest of any other employee in the office.

74. A In the reports of typists' speeds, the job analyst found some records that are kind of unusual.
    B. It says in the job analyst's report that some employees type with great speed.
    C. The job analyst found that, in reviewing the typists' work Reports, that some unusual typing speeds had been made.
    D. Work reports showing typing speeds include some typists who are unusual.
    E. In reviewing the typists' work reports, the job analyst found records of unusual typing speeds.

75. A It is quite possible that we shall reemploy anyone whose training fits them to do the work.
    B. It is probable that we shall reemploy those who have been trained to do the work.
    C. Such of our personnel that have been trained to do the work will be again employed.
    D. We expect to reemploy the ones who have had training enough that they can do the work.
    E. Some of these people have been trained

76. A He as well as his publisher were pleased with the success of the book.
    B. The success of the book pleased both his publisher and he.
    C. Both his publisher and he was pleased with the success of the book.
    D. Neither he or his publisher was disappointed with the success of the book.
    E. His publisher was as pleased as he with the success of the book.

77. A You have got to get rid of some of these people if you expect to have the quality of the work improve.
    B. The quality of the work would improve if they would leave fewer people do it.
    C. I believe it would be desirable to have fewer persons doing this work.
    D. If you had planned on employing fewer people than this to do the work, this situation would not have arose.
    E. Seeing how you have all those people on that work, it is not surprising that you have a great deal of confusion.

78. A She made lots of errors in her typed report, and which caused her to be repri-
        manded.
     B. The supervisor reprimanded the typist, whom she believed had made careless
         errors.
     C. Many errors were found in the report which she typed and could not disregard
         them.
     D. The typist would have corrected the errors, had she of known that the super-
         visor would see the report.
     E. The errors in the typed report were so numerous that they could hardly be over-
         looked.

79. A. This kind of a worker achieves success through patience.
     B. Success does not often come to men of this type except they who are patient.
     C. Because they are patient, these sort of workers usually achieve success.
     D. This worker has more patience than any man in his office.
     E. This kind of worker achieves success through patience.

80. A. I think that they will promote whoever has the best record.
     B. The firm would have liked to have promoted all employees with good records.
     C. Such of them that have the best records have excellent prospects of promotion.
     D. I feel sure they will give the promotion to whomever has the best record.
     E. Whoever they find to have the best record will, I think, be promoted.

KEY (CORRECT ANSWERS)

1. B	21. C	41. B	61. E
2. A	22. D	42. C	62. B
3. C	23. A	43. B	63. D
4. E	24. D	44. B	64. A
5. C	25. B	45. C	65. E
6. D	26. E	46. B	66. D
7. A	27. C	47. A	67. B
8. A	28. D	48. D	68. E
9. B	29. B	49. B	69. C
10. B	30. C	50. A	70. C
11. C	31. B	51. A	71. D
12. A	32. B	52. B	72. C
13. C	33. C	53. D	73. A
14. E	34. E	54. C	74. E
15. B	35. D	55. D	75. B
16. D	36. B	56. A	76. E
17. E	37. E	57. B	77. C
18. D	38. A	58. A	78. E
19. A	39. A	59. C	79. E
20. C	40. D	60. C	80. A

PREPARING WRITTEN MATERIAL

EXAMINATION SECTION
TEST 1

Questions 1-15.

DIRECTIONS: For each of Questions 1 through 15, select from the options given below the MOST applicable choice, and mark your answer accordingly.

    A. The sentence is correct.
    B. The sentence contains a spelling error *only.*
    C. The sentence contains an English grammar error *only.*
    D. The sentence contains both a spelling error and an English grammar error.

1. He is a very dependible person whom we expect will be an asset to this division.   1._____

2. An investigator often finds it necessary to be very diplomatic when conducting an interview.   2._____

3. Accurate detail is especially important if court action results from an investigation.   3._____

4. The report was signed by him and I since we conducted the investigation jointly.   4._____

5. Upon receipt of the complaint, an inquiry was begun.   5._____

6. An employee has to organize his time so that he can handle his workload efficiantly.   6._____

7. It was not apparant that anyone was living at the address given by the client.   7._____

8. According to regulations, there is to be at least three attempts made to locate the client.   8._____

9. Neither the inmate nor the correction officer was willing to sign a formal statement.   9._____

10. It is our opinion that one of the persons interviewed were lying.   10._____

11. We interviewed both clients and departmental personel in the course of this investigation.   11._____

12. It is concievable that further research might produce additional evidence.   12._____

13. There are too many occurences of this nature to ignore.   13._____

14. We cannot accede to the candidate's request.   14._____

15. The submission of overdue reports is the reason that there was a delay in completion of this investigation.   15._____

Questions 16-25.

DIRECTIONS: Each of Questions 16 through 25 may be classified under one of the following four categories:

    A. Faulty because of incorrect grammar or sentence structure
    B. Faulty because of incorrect punctuation
    C. Faulty because of incorrect spelling
    D. Correct

Examine each sentence carefully to determine under which of the above four options it is best classified. Then, in the space at the right, write the letter preceding the option which is the BEST of the four suggested above. Each incorrect sentence contains but one type of error. Consider a sentence to be correct if it contains none of the types of errors mentioned, even though there may be other correct ways of expressing the same thought.

16. Although the department's supply of scratch pads and stationary have diminished considerably, the allotment for our division has not been reduced.   16.____

17. You have not told us whom you wish to designate as your secretary.   17.____

18. Upon reading the minutes of the last meeting, the new proposal was taken up for consideration.   18.____

19. Before beginning the discussion, we locked the door as a precautionery measure.   19.____

20. The supervisor remarked, "Only those clerks, who perform routine work, are permitted to take a rest period."   20.____

21. Not only will this duplicating machine make accurate copies, but it will also produce a quantity of work equal to fifteen transcribing typists.   21.____

22. "Mr. Jones," said the supervisor, "we regret our inability to grant you an extention of your leave of absence."   22.____

23. Although the employees find the work monotonous and fatigueing, they rarely complain.   23.____

24. We completed the tabulation of the receipts on time despite the fact that Miss Smith our fastest operator was absent for over a week.   24.____

25. The reaction of the employees who attended the meeting, as well as the reaction of those who did not attend, indicates clearly that the schedule is satisfactory to everyone concerned.   25.____

KEY (CORRECT ANSWERS)

1.	D		11.	B
2.	A		12.	B
3.	A		13.	B
4.	C		14.	A
5.	A		15.	C
6.	B		16.	A
7.	B		17.	D
8.	C		18.	A
9.	A		19.	C
10.	C		20.	B

21.	A
22.	C
23.	C
24.	B
25.	D

TEST 2

Questions 1-15.

DIRECTIONS: Questions 1 through 15 consist of two sentences. Some are correct according to ordinary formal English usage. Others are incorrect because they contain errors in English usage, spelling, or punctuation. Consider a sentence correct if it contains no errors in English usage, spelling, or punctuation, even if there may be other ways of writing the sentence correctly. Mark your answer:

- A. If only sentence I is correct
- B. If only sentence II is correct
- C. If sentences I and II are correct
- D. If neither sentence I nor II is correct

1. I. The influence of recruitment efficiency upon administrative standards is readily apparant.
   II. Rapid and accurate thinking are an essential quality of the police officer.

   1.____

2. I. The administrator of a police department is constantly confronted by the demands of subordinates for increased personnel in their respective units.
   II. Since a chief executive must work within well-defined fiscal limits, he must weigh the relative importance of various requests.

   2.____

3. I. The two men whom the police arrested for a parking violation were wanted for robbery in three states.
   II. Strong executive control from the top to the bottom of the enterprise is one of the basic principals of police administration.

   3.____

4. I. When he gave testimony unfavorable to the defendant loyalty seemed to mean very little.
   II. Having run off the road while passing a car, the patrolman gave the driver a traffic ticket.

   4.____

5. I. The judge ruled that the defendant's conversation with his doctor was a priviliged communication.
   II. The importance of our training program is widely recognized; however, fiscal difficulties limit the program's effectiveness.

   5.____

6. I. Despite an increase in patrol coverage, there were less arrests for crimes against property this year.
   II. The investigators could hardly have expected greater cooperation from the public.

   6.____

7. I. Neither the patrolman nor the witness could identify the defendant as the driver of the car.
   II. Each of the officers in the class received their certificates at the completion of the course.

   7.____

8.   I.   The new commander made it clear that those kind of procedures would no longer   8.____
be permitted.
     II.   Giving some weight to performance records is more advisable then making pro-
motions solely on the basis of test scores.

9.   I.   A deputy sheriff must ascertain whether the debtor, has any property.   9.____
     II.   A good deputy sheriff does not cause histerical excitement when he executes a
process.

10.   I.   Having learned that he has been assigned a judgment debtor, the deputy sheriff   10.____
should call upon him.
     II.   The deputy sheriff may seize and remove property without requiring a bond.

11.   I.   If legal procedures are not observed, the resulting contract is not enforseable.   11.____
     II.   If the directions from the creditor's attorney are not in writing, the deputy sheriff
should request a letter of instructions from the attorney.

12.   I.   The deputy sheriff may confer with the defendant and may enter this defendants'   12.____
place of business.
     II.   A deputy sheriff must ascertain from the creditor's attorney whether the debtor
has any property against which he may proceede.

13.   I.   The sheriff has a right to do whatever is reasonably necessary for the purpose of   13.____
executing the order of the court.
     II.   The written order of the court gives the sheriff general authority and he is gov-
erned in his acts by a very simple principal.

14.   I.   Either the patrolman or his sergeant are always ready to help the public.   14.____
     II.   The sergeant asked the patrolman when he would finish the report.

15.   I.   The injured man could not hardly talk.   15.____
     II.   Every officer had ought to hand in their reports on time.

Questions 16-25.

DIRECTIONS: For each of the sentences given below, numbered 16 through 25, select from
the following choices the MOST correct choice and print your choice in the
space at the right. Select as your answer:

     A.   If the statement contains an unnecessary word or expression
     B.   If the statement contains a slang term or expression ordinarily not
acceptable in government report writing
     C.   If the statement contains an old-fashioned word or expression, where a
concrete, plain term would be more useful
     D.   If the statement contains no major faults

16.   Every one of us should try harder   16.____

17.   Yours of the first instant has been received.   17.____

18.   We will have to do a real snow job on him.   18.____

19.   I shall contact him next Thursday.   19.____

20. None of us were invited to the meeting with the community.   20.____

21. We got this here job to do.   21.____

22. She could not help but see the mistake in the checkbook.   22.____

23. Don't bug the Director about the report.   23.____

24. I beg to inform you that your letter has been received.   24.____

25. This project is all screwed up.   25.____

KEY (CORRECT ANSWERS)

1.	D		11.	B
2.	C		12.	D
3.	A		13.	A
4.	D		14.	D
5.	B		15.	D
6.	B		16.	D
7.	A		17.	C
8.	D		18.	B
9.	D		19.	D
10.	C		20.	D

21.	B
22.	D
23.	B
24.	C
25.	B

TEST 3

DIRECTIONS: Questions 1 through 25 are sentences taken from reports. Some are correct according to ordinary formal English usage. Others are incorrect because they contain errors in English usage, spelling, or punctuation. Consider a sentence correct if it contains no errors in English usage, spelling, or punctuation, even if there may be other ways of writing the sentence correctly. Mark your answer:

    A.   If only sentence I is correct
    B.   If only sentence II is correct
    C.   If sentences I and II are correct
    D.   If neither sentence I nor II is correct.

1.   I.   The Neighborhood Police Team Commander and Team Patrol- men are encouraged to give to the public the widest possible verbal and written disemination of information regarding the existence and purposes of the program.
     II.   The police must be vitally interelated with every segment of the public they serve.

2.   I.   If social gambling, prostitution, and other vices are to be prohibited, the law makers should provide the manpower and method for enforcement.
     II.   In addition to checking on possible crime locations such as hallways, roofs yards and other similar locations, Team Patrolmen are encouraged to make known their presence to members of the community.

3.   I.   The Neighborhood Police Team Commander is authorized to secure, the cooperation of local publications, as well as public and private agencies, to further the goals of the program.
     II.   Recruitment from social minorities is essential to effective police work among minorities and meaningful relations with them.

4.   I.   The Neighborhood Police Team Commander and his men have the responsibility for providing patrol service within the sector territory on a twenty-four hour basis.
     II.   While the patrolman was walking his beat at midnight he noticed that the clothing stores' door was partly open.

5.   I.   Authority is granted to the Neighborhood Police Team to device tactics for coping with the crime in the sector.
     II.   Before leaving the scene of the accident, the patrolman drew a map showing the positions of the automobiles and indicated the time of the accident as 10 M. in the morning.

6.   I.   The Neighborhood Police Team Commander and his men must be kept apprised of conditions effecting their sector.
     II.   Clear, continuous communication with every segment of the public served based on the realization of mutual need and founded on trust and confidence is the basis for effective law enforcement.

7. I. The irony is that the police are blamed for the laws they enforce when they are doing their duty.
    II. The Neighborhood Police Team Commander is authorized to prepare and distribute literature with pertinent information telling the public whom to contact for assistance.

7.____

8. I. The day is not far distant when major parts of the entire police compliment will need extensive college training or degrees.
    II. Although driving under the influence of alcohol is a specific charge in making arrests, drunkeness is basically a health and social problem.

8.____

9. I. If a deputy sheriff finds that property he has to attach is located on a ship, he should notify his supervisor.
    II. Any contract that tends to interfere with the administration of justice is illegal.

9.____

10. I. A mandate or official order of the court to the sheriff or other officer directs it to take into possession property of the judgment debtor.
    II. Tenancies from month-to-month, week-to-week, and sometimes year-to-year are termenable.

10.____

11. I. A civil arrest is an arrest pursuant to an order issued by a court in civil litigation.
    II. In a criminal arrest, a defendant is arrested for a crime he is alleged to have committed.

11.____

12. I. Having taken a defendant into custody, there is a complete restraint of personal liberty.
    II. Actual force is unnecessary when a deputy sheriff makes an arrest.

12.____

13. I. When a husband breaches a separation agreement by failing to supply to the wife the amount of money to be paid to her periodically under the agreement, the same legal steps may be taken to enforce his compliance as in any other breach of contract.
    II. Having obtained the writ of attachment, the plaintiff is then in the advantageous position of selling the very property that has been held for him by the sheriff while he was obtaining a judgment.

13.____

14. I. Being locked in his desk, the investigator felt sure that the records would be safe.
    II. The reason why the witness changed his statement was because he had been threatened.

14.____

15. I. The investigation had just began then an important witness disappeared.
    II. The check that had been missing was located and returned to its owner, Harry Morgan, a resident of Suffolk County, New York.

15.____

16. I. A supervisor will find that the establishment of standard procedures enables his staff to work more efficiently.
    II. An investigator hadn't ought to give any recommendations in his report if he is in doubt.

16.____

17. I. Neither the investigator nor his supervisor is ready to interview the witnesses.
    II. Interviewing has been and always will be an important asset in investigation.

17.____

18.   I.   One of the investigator's reports has been forwarded to the wrong person.   18.____
      II.   The investigator stated that he was not familiar with those kind of cases.

19.   I.   Approaching the victim of the assault, two large bruises were noticed by me.   19.____
      II.   The prisoner was arrested for assault, resisting arrest, and use of a deadly weapon.

20.   I.   A copy of the orders, which had been prepared by the captain, was given to each   20.____
        patrolman.
      II.   It's always necessary to inform an arrested person of his constitutional rights before asking him any questions.

21.   I.   To prevent further bleeding, I applied a tourniquet to the wound.   21.____
      II.   John Rano a senior officer was on duty at the time of the accident.

22.   I.   Limiting the term "property" to tangible property, in the criminal mischief setting,   22.____
        accords with prior case law holding that only tangible property came within the purview of the offense of malicious mischief.
      II.   Thus, a person who intentionally destroys the property of another, but under an honest belief that he has title to such property, cannot be convicted of criminal mischief under the Revised Penal Law.

23.   I.   Very early in it's history, New York enacted statutes from time to time punishing,   23.____
        either as a felony or as a misdemeanor, malicious injuries to various kinds of property: piers, booms, dams, bridges, etc.
      II.   The application of the statute is necessarily restricted to trespassory takings with larcenous intent: namely with intent permanently or virtually permanently to "appropriate" property or "deprive" the owner of its use.

24.   I.   Since the former Penal Law did not define the instruments of forgery in a general   24.____
        fashion, its crime of forgery was held to be narrower than the common law offense in this respect and to embrace only those instruments explicitly specified in the substantive provisions.
      II.   After entering the barn through an open door for the purpose of stealing, it was closed by the defendants.

25.   I.   The use of fire or explosives to destroy tangible property is proscribed by the crim-   25.____
        inal mischief provisions of the Revised Penal Law.
      II.   The defendant's taking of a taxicab for the immediate purpose of affecting his escape did not constitute grand larceny.

KEY (CORRECT ANSWERS)

1.	D		11.	C
2.	D		12.	B
3.	B		13.	C
4.	A		14.	D
5.	D		15.	B
6.	D		16.	A
7.	C		17.	C
8.	D		18.	A
9.	C		19.	B
10.	D		20.	C

21.	A
22.	C
23.	B
24.	A
25.	A

———

TEST 4

Questions 1-4.

DIRECTIONS: Each of the two sentences in Questions 1 through 4 may be correct or may contain errors in punctuation, capitalization, or grammar. Mark your answer:

    A. If there is an error only in sentence I
    B. If there is an error only in sentence II
    C. If there is an error in both sentences I and II
    D. If both sentences are correct.

1.   I. It is very annoying to have a pencil sharpener, which is not in working order.   1.____
    II. Patrolman Blake checked the door of Joe's Restaurant and found that the lock has been jammed.

2.   I. When you are studying a good textbook is important.   2.____
    II. He said he would divide the money equally between you and me.

3.   I. Since he went on the city council a year ago, one of his primary concerns has been   3.____
    safety in the streets.
    II. After waiting in the doorway for about 15 minutes, a black sedan appeared.

Questions 5-9.

DIRECTIONS: Each of the sentences in Questions 5 through 9 may be classified under one of the following four categories:
    A. Faulty because of incorrect grammar
    B. Faulty because of incorrect punctuation
    C. Faulty because of incorrect capitalization or incorrect spelling
    D. Correct

Examine each sentence carefully to determine under which of the above four options it is BEST classified. Then, in the space at the right, print the capitalized letter preceding the option which is the BEST of the four suggested above. Each faulty sentence contains but one type of error. Consider a sentence to be correct if it contains none of the types of errors mentioned, even though there may be other correct ways of expressing the same thought.

5. They told both he and I that the prisoner had escaped.   5.____

6. Any superior officer, who, disregards the just complaints of his subordinates, is remiss in   6.____
the performance of his duty.

7. Only those members of the national organization who resided in the Middle west   7.____
attended the conference in Chicago.

8. We told him to give the investigation assignment to whoever was available.   8.____

9. Please do not disappoint and embarass us by not appearing in court.   9.____

Questions 10-14.

DIRECTIONS: Each of Questions 10 through 14 consists of three sentences lettered A, B, and C. In each of these questions, one of the sentences may contain an error in grammar, sentence structure, or punctuation, or all three sentences may be correct. If one of the sentences in a question contains an error in grammar, sentence structure, or punctuation, print in the space at the right the capital letter preceding the sentence which contains the error. If all three sentences are correct, print the letter D.

10.   A.   Mr. Smith appears to be less competent than I in performing these duties.   10.____
       B.   The supervisor spoke to the employee, who had made the error, but did not reprimand him.
       C.   When he found the book lying on the table, he immediately notified the owner.

11.   A.   Being locked in the desk, we were certain that the papers would not be taken.   11.____
       B.   It wasn't I who dictated the telegram; I believe it was Eleanor.
       C.   You should interview whoever comes to the office today.

12.   A.   The clerk was instructed to set the machine on the table before summoning the   12.____
             manager.
       B.   He said that he was not familiar with those kind of activities.
       C.   A box of pencils, in addition to erasers and blotters, was included in the shipment
             of supplies.

13.   A.   The supervisor remarked, "Assigning an employee to the proper type of work is not   13.____
             always easy."
       B.   The employer found that each of the applicants were qualified to perform the
             duties of the position.
       C.   Any competent student is permitted to take this course if he obtains the consent
             of the instructor.

14.   A.   The prize was awarded to the employee whom the judges believed to be most   14.____
             deserving.
       B.   Since the instructor believes this book is the better of the two, he is recommend-
             ing it for use in the school.
       C.   It was obvious to the employees that the completion of the task by the scheduled
             date would require their working overtime.

Questions 15-21.

DIRECTIONS: In answering Questions 15 through 21, choose the sentence which is BEST from the point of view of English usage suitable for a business report.

15.   A.   The client's receiving of public assistance checks at two different addresses were   15.____
              disclosed by the investigation.
       B.   The investigation disclosed that the client was receiving public assistance
              checks at two different addresses.
       C.   The client was found out by the investigation to be receiving public assistance
              checks at two different addresses.
       D.   The client has been receiving public assistance checks at two different
              addresses, disclosed the investigation.

16.   A.   The investigation of complaints are usually handled by this unit, which deals with   16.____
              internal security problems in the department.
       B.   This unit deals with internal security problems in the department usually investi-
              gating complaints.
       C.   Investigating complaints is this unit's job, being that it handles internal security
              problems in the department.
       D.   This unit deals with internal security problems in the department and usually
              investigates complaints.

17.   A.   The delay in completing this investigation was caused by difficulty in obtaining the   17.____
              required documents from the candidate.
       B.   Because of difficulty in obtaining the required documents from the candidate is
              the reason that there was a delay in completing this investigation.
       C.   Having had difficulty in obtaining the required documents from the candidate,
              there was a delay in completing this investigation.
       D.   Difficulty in obtaining the required documents from the candidate had the affect
              of delaying the completion of this investigation.

18.   A.   This report, together with documents supporting our recommendation, are being   18.____
              submitted for your approval.
       B.   Documents supporting our recommendation is being submitted with the report
              for your approval.
       C.   This report, together with documents supporting our recommendation, is being
              submitted for your approval.
       D.   The report and documents supporting our recommendation is being submitted
              for your approval.

19.   A.   The chairman himself, rather than his aides, has reviewed the report.   19.____
       B.   The chairman himself, rather than his aides, have reviewed the report.
       C.   The chairmen, not the aide, has reviewed the report.
       D.   The aide, not the chairmen, have reviewed the report.

20.   A.   Various proposals were submitted but the decision is not been made.   20.____
       B.   Various proposals has been submitted but the decision has not been made.
       C.   Various proposals were submitted but the decision is not been made.
       D.   Various proposals have been submitted but the decision has not been made.

21.   A.   Everyone were rewarded for his successful attempt.   21.____
       B.   They were successful in their attempts and each of them was rewarded.
       C.   Each of them are rewarded for their successful attempts.
       D.   The reward for their successful attempts were made to each of them.

22. The following is a paragraph from a request for departmental recognition consisting of five numbered sentences submitted to a Captain for review. These sentences may or may not have errors in spelling, grammar, and punctuation:

22.____

1. The officers observed the subject Mills surreptitiously remove a wallet from the woman's handbag and entered his automobile. 2. As they approached Mills, he looked in their direction and drove away. 3. The officers pursued in their car. 4. Mills executed a series of complicated manuvers to evade the pursuing officers. 5. At the corner of Broome and Elizabeth Streets, Mills stopped the car, got out, raised his hands and surrendered to the officers.

Which one of the following BEST classifies the above with regard to spelling, grammar and punctuation?

    A. 1, 2, and 3 are correct, but 4 and 5 have errors.
    B. 2, 3, and 5 are correct, but 1 and 4 have errors.
    C. 3, 4, and 5 are correct, but 1 and 2 have errors.
    D. 1, 2, 3, and 5 are correct, but 4 has errors.

23. The one of the following sentences which is grammatically PREFERABLE to the others is:

23.____

    A. Our engineers will go over your blueprints so that you may have no problems in construction.
    B. For a long time he had been arguing that we, not he, are to blame for the confusion.
    C. I worked on this automobile for two hours and still cannot find out what is wrong with it.
    D. Accustomed to all kinds of hardships, fatigue seldom bothers veteran policemen.

24. The MOST accurate of the following sentences is:

24.____

    A. The commissioner, as well as his deputy and various bureau heads, were present.
    B. A new organization of employers and employees have been formed.
    C. One or the other of these men have been selected.
    D. The number of pages in the book is enough to discourage a reader.

25. The MOST accurate of the following sentences is:

25.____

    A. Between you and me, I think he is the better man.
    B. He was believed to be me.
    C. Is it us that you wish to see?
    D. The winners are him and her.

KEY (CORRECT ANSWERS)

1. C	11. A
2. A	12. B
3. C	13. B
4. B	14. D
5. A	15. B
6. B	16. D
7. C	17. A
8. D	18. C
9. C	19. A
10. B	20. D

21. B
22. B
23. A
24. D
25. A

REPORT WRITING
EXAMINATION SECTION
TEST 1

DIRECTIONS: Each question or incomplete statement is followed by several suggested answers or completions. Select the one that BEST answers the question or completes the statement. *PRINT THE LETTER OF THE CORRECT ANSWER IN THE SPACE AT THE RIGHT.*

Questions 1-4.

DIRECTIONS: Questions 1 through 4 are based on the following report relating to a demonstration. The report consists of twenty-four numbered sentences, some of which may not be correct or consistent with the principles of good police report writing.

(1) At 1000 hours this date, the undersigned received notification from Lieutenant Thomas Yale, assigned to Patrol Bureau Headquarters, that a demonstration was in progress at Pomonok Houses. (2) Responded to the Management Office, arriving at 1025 hours. (3) Upon arrival, observed approximately 200 persons picketing in front of the building which houses the Management Office. (4) Demonstrators were carrying placards calling for increased police protection. (5) Upon entry into the interior of the Management Office, observed approximately 40 persons "sitting in" and disrupting normal office operation. (6) The manager, Ms. Roberts, was being detained within her private office by four demonstrators, who refused to allow her to leave. (7) The undersigned immediately deployed the available patrol force: one Lieutenant, one Sergeant, and four Police Officers. (8) The Sergeant and two Police Officers were directed to secure the front door of the facility, with instructions to allow persons to leave but not to re-enter. (9) The Lieutenant and two Police Officers were directed to maintain order with respect to the demonstrators in front of the building. (10) The undersigned was able to ascertain that the demonstration was being led by Ann Thomas, a tenant of Building #2, and the leader of an insurgent tenant group seeking to depose the elected head of the recognized tenants association, Mary Miller.

(11) The remaining Police Officer and the undersigned entered the manager's private office and engaged in conversation with the demonstrators, including the above-mentioned Ann Thomas. (12) The undersigned impressed upon Ms. Thomas that she and her followers were in violation of law and subject to arrest. (13) Ms. Thomas was urged to call off the demonstration and to select a representative group of six tenants for the purpose of a meeting with the project manager and the undersigned, in order to discuss remedial measures which might improve conditions at the location. (14) Ms. Thomas was at first reluctant but finally agreed to comply with the proposal made by the undersigned. (15) At 1115 hours, Ms. Thomas addressed the demonstrators and requested that all leave the area, except for the six selected for the meeting, including Mary Miller and Ann Thomas. (16) After considerable discussion, the demonstrators complied with her request. (17) At 1200 hours, a meeting was convened in the Pomonok Community Center and in attendance were the project manager, Ms. Robert; Mary Miller, President of the Tenants Association; Ann Thomas; four other project residents; and the undersigned.

(18) Upon inquiry as to the numerical strength of the police contingent at Pomonok, the undersigned advised that with the officers assigned, the development received scheduled coverage by scooter or foot patrol on an around-the-clock basis, except for the first platoon on Wednesdays when alternate days off allowed for a chart change. (19) This information was not well received by the tenants who demanded that the number of police officers assigned be doubled to combat the alleged crime conditions. (20) In addition, the Department's Task Force and Detective Bureau have suffered manpower losses. (21) The meeting concluded at 1300 hours with a statement by Ann Thomas to the effect that if conditions did not improve within a reasonable period of time, further demonstrations would be held. (22) The undersigned advised that this was not possible due to existing manpower shortage as a result of fiscal problems. (23) The undersigned mentioned that the current budget crisis has forced a severe reduction in the number of automobiles which may be purchased by the Department. (24) The undersigned concluded by stating that, notwithstanding the aforementioned reductions in manpower availability, necessary steps would be taken to assign a limited number of plainclothes officers to the development, on a sporadic basis, in an effort to effect summary arrests.

1. Which one of the following sentences contains materials CONTRADICTED by other information given in the report?
    A. 1   B. 6   C. 11   D. 17   1.____

2. Of the following, which would be the MOST logical sequence for sentences 20 through 24 of the report?   2.____
    A. 23, 20, 21, 22, 24   B. 22, 23, 20, 24, 21
    C. 20, 24, 22, 23, 21   D. 23, 20, 22, 21, 24

3. Which one of the following sentences contain material which is LEAST relevant to this report?   3.____
    A. 20   B. 21   C. 23   D. 24

4. Which one of the following sentences is LEAST clear?   4.____
    A. 8   B. 13   C. 16   D. 18

KEY (CORRECT ANSWERS)

1. C
2. B
3. C
4. D

TEST 2

DIRECTIONS: Each question or incomplete statement is followed by several suggested answers or completions. Select the one that BEST answers the question or completes the statement. *PRINT THE LETTER OF THE CORRECT ANSWER IN THE SPACE AT THE RIGHT.*

Questions 1-3.

DIRECTIONS: Questions 1 through 3 are based on the following report relating to a Tenants' Association meeting attended by a Sergeant under your command. The report consists of ten numbered sentences, some of which may not be correct or consistent with the principles of good report writing.

      (1) Mrs. Thelma Cohen of Building #5 started the meeting by complaining that young children continually loiter in and about the lobby entrance of her building. (2) The undersigned was directed to attend the monthly Tenants' Association meeting by the Division Commanding Officer. (3) The meeting, scheduled to start at 2000 hours, actually got under way at 2040 hours. (4) Present were Captain Gary Jones of the local N.Y.C. Police Department Precinct; Mr. Arnold, the project superintendent; Ms. Chester, the project manager; a group of tenants; and the undersigned appearing on behalf of this Department. (5) Mr. Tom Bonny, Building Captain of Building #2, stated that conditions in his resident building were improving. (6) Ms. Maria Gonzalez of Building #1, complained that vandalism continues to run rampant in her building. (7) She added that the Sanitation Department had not yet complied with previous promises made to the tenants. (8) Mrs. Yvonne Brown complained that mailbox vandalism continues to be a problem in Building #8. (9) The undersigned, when called upon to speak, advised that necessary steps would be taken to establish special post conditions in Buildings 1, 2, and 8, in an effort to suppress the conditions alleged to be existing. (10) The meeting concluded, with pledges of future cooperation in matters of mutual concern, at 2200 hours.

1.   Of the following, the MOST logical sequence for the first four sentences of the   1.____
     report is:
     A. 3, 2, 4, 1   B. 3, 1, 4, 2   C. 2, 3, 4, 1   D. 4, 1, 3, 2

2.   Which one of the following sentences contains material which is LEAST   2.____
     relevant to the report?
     A. 1   B. 2   C. 5   D. 7

3.   Based on the report, the Sergeant concerned failed to respond to the   3.____
     complaint made by which tenant?
     A. Bonny   B. Cohen   C. Gonzalez   D. Brown

KEY (CORRECT ANSWERS)

1. C
2. D
3. B

TEST 3

DIRECTIONS: Each question or incomplete statement is followed by several suggested answers or completions. Select the one that BEST answers the question or completes the statement. *PRINT THE LETTER OF THE CORRECT ANSWER IN THE SPACE AT THE RIGHT.*

Questions 1-5.

DIRECTIONS: Questions 1 through 5 are based on the following report relating to an investigation of a civilian complaint against a member of the force. The report consists of thirty-eight numbered sentences, some of which may not be correct or consistent with the principles of good police report writing.

(1) The complainant was interviewed by the undersigned in the complainant's resident apartment on 6/1 at 1500 hours. (2) At 1420 hours, 6/1, notification was received by the undersigned for investigation by Sergeant Daniel Andrews. (3) On 6/1 at 1400 hours, Ms. Geraldine Rich, F/B/39 (T), resident of 429 Dumont Avenue, Brooklyn, New York, Van Dyke Houses, telephone the Headquarters Desk Supervisor, Sergeant Andrews, and lodged a civilian complaint against Police Officer Robert Boyle, #2999, assigned to the Brownsville Complex. (4) During the interview, Ms. Rich alleged the following:

(5) On 6/1 at 0900 hours, her daughter, Jane Rich, F/B/17, who lives with her, was arrested by Police Officer Boyle in front of their resident building and charged with Disorderly Conduct, Menacing, and Possession of a Dangerous Instrument. (6) In the course of effecting the arrest, Police Officer Boyle struck her daughter with his night stick, inflicting damage thereto. (7) Her daughter was treated at Kings County Hospital by Dr. Cohen, who administered twelve sutures to the right cheek and released the patient. (8) Ms. Rich did not witness the incident but was made aware of it when she responded to the hospital, at the request of hospital personnel, for the purpose of signing necessary release forms. (9) Ms. Rich expressed outrage at the need for a police officer, 6'2" tall, to strike her daughter, 5'1" tall, with his night stick, under these circumstances.

(10) Jane Rich was interviewed, in the presence of her mother, at 1520 hours, 6/1. (11) She stated the information that follows:

(12) At the time and place of occurrence, in the company of two classmates, Sarah Moore, Apartment 121, and Mary Williams, Apartment 10J, of 429 Dumont Avenue, she was approached by Police Officer Boyle. (13) He told them that they were blocking the building door in violation of law and directed that they cease immediately. (14) Sarah and Mary immediately complied by walking a distance of approximately six feet from the building entrance. (15) Jane stopped to tie her shoe, whereupon the officer advised her that she was under arrest. (16) She started to walk away and join her friends, thinking that the officer was joking. (17) Police Officer Boyle approached the three girls and roughly grabbed Jane by the right wrist. (18) She, fearing for her safety, removed a hair brush from her pocket and pulled her wrist from the officer's grasp. (19) She retreated two or three steps and stated to the officer, "Let me call my mother." (20) He took several rapid steps toward her and struck her across the face with his stick. (21) She fell to the ground, was handcuffed, and was taken to the Police Room on Stone Avenue. (22) An ambulance responded and she went to the hospital. (23) After her release from the hospital she appeared in court this date, pleaded not guilty, and was released to the custody of her mother. (24) At 1600 hours, 6/1, the undersigned interviewed Mary Moore in her resident apartment. (25) She corroborated, in essence, the version given by Jane Rich. (26) At

1615 hours, 6/1, the undersigned interviewed Sarah Williams in her resident apartment. (27) She agreed in substance with the statements given by Jane and Mary. (28) She added that this was yet another instance of nation-wide oppression inflicted upon the poor by the power structure. (29) At 1700 hours, 6/1, Police Officer Boyle was interviewed by the undersigned, after he was advised of his rights. (30) It was noted that Police Officer Boyle was well groomed and articulate. (31) The officer refused to give a written statement to the undersigned. (32) He stated that investigations of this nature were geared towards the proliferation of a society that had lost hope and that he would not contribute to it. (33) Captain Thomas Davis, the Patrol Division Commander, suspended Police Officer Boyle at 1730 hours. (34) A determination as to the allegation of excessive use of force rests upon the statements on the one hand of Jane Rich and Mary Moore, as opposed to the silence on the part of the officer. (35) Sarah Williams' statement must be discounted in view of her hostility and biases. (36) The preponderance of evidence leads to a finding of "substantiated" with respect to the allegation. (37) Criminal aspects will be further pursued with the Kings County District Attorney's office. (38) Disciplinary aspects and recommendations will follow in a subsequent report.

1. Of the following, which would be the MOST logical sequence for the first four sentences of the report?   1.____
   A. 3, 2, 1, 4   B. 2, 3, 1, 4   C. 1, 4, 2, 3   D. 2, 1, 4, 3

2. Which one of the following sentences is AMBIGUOUS?   2.____
   A. 3   B. 5   C. 6   D. 9

3. Which one of the following sentences contains material which is CONTRADICTED by other information given in the report?   3.____
   A. 8   B. 14   C. 21   D. 24

4. Which one of the following sentences contains a conclusion which is NOT supported by facts given in the report?   4.____
   A. 9   B. 18   C. 34   D. 35

5. Which one of the following sentences from the report contains material which is LEAST relevant to the report?   5.____
   A. 8   B. 13   C. 20   D. 30

KEY (CORRECT ANSWERS)

1. A
2. C
3. D
4. D
5. D

ARITHMETICAL REASONING
EXAMINATION SECTION
TEST 1

DIRECTIONS: Each question or incomplete statement is followed by several suggested answers or completions. Select the one that BEST answers the question or completes the statement. *PRINT THE LETTER OF THE CORRECT ANSWER IN THE SPACE AT THE RIGHT.*

1. Multiply $38.85 by 2; then subtract $27.90.
   The CORRECT answer is:

   A. $21.90   B. $48.70   C. $49.80   D. $50.70

   1.____

2. Add $53.66, $9.27, and $18.75; then divide by 2.
   The CORRECT answer is:

   A. $35.84   B. $40.34   C. $40.84   D. $41.34

   2.____

3. Out of 192 inmates in a certain cellblock, 96 are to go on a work detail and another 32 are to report to a vocational class. All the rest are to remain in the cellblock. How many inmates should be left on the cellblock?

   A. 48   B. 64   C. 86   D. 128

   3.____

4. Assume that you are responsible for seeing that the right number of utensils are counted out for a meal. You need enough utensils for 620 men. One fork and one spoon are needed for each man. In addition, one ladle is needed for each group of 20 men. How many utensils will be needed altogether?

   A. 1,240   B. 1,271   C. 1,550   D. 1,860

   4.____

5. Assume that you are supervising the inmates who are assigned to a dishwashing detail. There is an inverse relationship between the amount of time it takes to do all the dishwashing and the number of inmates who are washing dishes. When two inmates are washing dishes, the job takes six hours.
   If there are four inmates washing dishes, how long should the job take?
   _____ hour(s).

   A. 1   B. 2   C. 3   D. 4

   5.____

6. A certain cellblock has 240 inmates. From 8 A.M. to 9 A.M. on March 25, 120 inmates were assigned to cleanup work and 25 inmates were sent for physical examinations. All the others remained in their cells.
   How many inmates should have been in their cells during this hour?

   A. 65   B. 85   C. 95   D. 105

   6.____

7. There were 254 inmates in a certain cellblock at the beginning of the day. At 9:30 A.M., 12 inmates were checked out to the dispensary. At 10:00 A.M., 113 inmates were checked out to work details. At 10:30 A.M., 3 inmates were checked out to another cellblock.
   How many inmates were present in this cellblock at 10:45 A.M. if none of the inmates who were checked out had returned?

   A. 116   B. 126   C. 136   D. 226

   7.____

8. There were 242 inmates in a certain cellblock at the beginning of the day. At 9:00 A.M., 116 inmates were checked out to a recreational program. At 9:15, 36 inmates were checked out to an educational program. At 9:30, 78 inmates were checked out on a work detail. By 10:15, the only inmates who had returned were 115 inmates who had been checked back in from the recreational program.
A count made at 10:15 should show that the number of inmates present in the cell-block is

8.____

   A. 127   B. 128   C. 135   D. 137

9. If an officer's weekly salary is increased from $400 to $450, then the percent of increase is _____ percent.

9.____

   A. 10   B. 11 1/9   C. 12 1/2   D. 20

10. Suppose that one-half the officers in a department have served for more than ten years and one-third have served for more than 15 years.
Then, the fraction of officers who have served between ten and fifteen years is

10.____

   A. 1/3   B. 1/5   C. 1/6   D. 1/12

11. In a prison, there are four floors on which prisoners are housed. The top floor houses one-quarter of the inmates, the bottom floor houses one-sixth of the inmates, and one-third are houses on the second floor. The rest of the inmates are housed on the third floor.
If there are 90 inmates housed on the third floor, the TOTAL number of inmates housed on all four floors together is

11.____

   A. 270   B. 360   C. 450   D. 540

12. Assume that you are in charge of supervising the laundry sorting and counting. You expect that on a certain day there will be nearly 7,000 items to be sorted and counted. If one inmate can sort and count 500 items in an hour, how many inmates are needed to sort all 7,000 items in one hour?

12.____

   A. 2   B. 5   C. 7   D. 14

13. A carpentry course is being given for inmates who want to learn a skill. The course will be taught in several different groups. Each group should contain at least 12 but not more than 16 men. The smaller the group, the better, as long as there are at least 12 men per group.
If 66 inmates are going to take the course, they should be divided into _____ groups of _____.

13.____

   A. 4; 16 men
   B. 4; 13 men and 1 group of 14 men
   C. 3; 13 men and 2 groups of 14 men
   D. 6; 11 men

14. Of the 100 inmates in a certain cellblock, one-half were assigned to cleanup work, and one-fifth were assigned to work in the laundry.
How many inmates were NOT assigned for cleanup work or laundry work?

14.____

   A. 30   B. 40   C. 50   D. 60

15. A certain cellblock has a maximum capacity of 250 inmates. On March 26, there were 200 inmates housed in the cellblock. 12 inmates were added on that day, and 17 inmates were added on the following day. No inmates left on either day.
How many more inmates could this cellblock have accommodated on the second day? 15.____

    A. 11   B. 16   C. 21   D. 28

16. Suppose that ten percent of those who commit serious crimes are convicted and that fifteen percent of those convicted are sentenced for more than 3 years.
The percentage of those committing serious crimes who are sentenced for more than 3 years is _____ percent. 16.____

    A. 15   B. 1.5   C. .15   D. .015

17. Assume that there are 1,100 employees in a city agency. Of these, 15 percent are officers, 80 percent of whom are attorneys; of the attorneys, two-fifths have been with the agency over five years.
Then, the number of officers who are attorneys and have over five years experience with the agency is MOST NEARLY 17.____

    A. 45   B. 53   C. 132   D. 165

18. An employee who has 500 cartons of supplies to pack can pack them at the rate of 50 an hour. After this employee has worked for half an hour, he is joined by another employee who can pack 45 cartons an hour.
Assuming that both employees can maintain their respective rates of speed, then the TOTAL number of hours required to pack all the cartons is 18.____

    A. 4 1/2   B. 5   C. 5 1/2   D. 6 1/2

19. Thirty-six officers can complete an assignment in 22 days. Assuming that all officers work at the same rate of speed, the number of officers that would be needed to complete this assignment in 12 days is 19.____

    A. 42   B. 54   C. 66   D. 72

Questions 20-22.

DIRECTIONS: Questions 20 through 22 are to be answered on the basis of the table below. Data for certain categories have been omitted from the table. You are to calculate the missing numbers if needed to answer the questions.

	2007	2008	Numerical Increase
Correction Officers	1,226	1,347	
Court Attendants		529	34
Deputy Sheriffs	38	40	
Supervisors			
	2,180	2,414	

20. The number in the *Supervisors* group in 2007 was MOST NEARLY   20._____

    A.   500   B.   475   C.   450   D.   425

21. The LARGEST percentage increase from 2007 to 2008 was in the group of   21._____

    A.   Correction Officers   B.   Court Attendants
    C.   Deputy Sheriffs   D.   Supervisors

22. In 2008, the ratio of the number of Correction Officers to the total of the other three cate-   22._____
    gories of employees was MOST NEARLY

    A.   1:1   B.   2:1   C.   3:1   D.   4:1

23. If an officer's weekly salary is increased from $640.00 to $720.00, then the percent of   23._____
    increase is _____ percent.

    A.   10   B.   11 1/9   C.   12 1/2   D.   20

24. Suppose that one-half the officers in a department have served for more than ten years   24._____
    and one-third have served for more than 15 years.
    If there are 150 officers In the department, how many have served less than 10 years?

    A.   25   B.   50   C.   75   D.   100

25. Moving radar can allow a trooper to clock the speed of an oncoming vehicle.   25._____
    If the radar shows a combined speed of 140 mph and the patrol car Is cruising at
    65mph, how fast is the oncoming vehicle traveling? _____ mph.

    A.   205   B.   85   C.   75   D.   65

KEY (CORRECT ANSWERS)

1.	C		11.	B
2.	C		12.	D
3.	B		13.	B
4.	B		14.	A
5.	C		15.	C
6.	C		16.	B
7.	B		17.	B
8.	A		18.	C
9.	C		19.	C
10.	C		20.	D

21.	D
22.	A
23.	C
24.	A
25.	C

SOLUTIONS TO PROBLEMS

1. ($38.85)(2) = $77.70, and $77.70 - $27.90 = $49.80

2. $53.66 + $9.27 + $18.75 = $81.68, and $81.68 ÷ 2 = $40.84

3. 192 - 96 - 32 = 64 left in the cellblock

4. Number of forks and spoons combined = (620)(2) = 1240

    Number of ladles = 620 ÷ 20 = 31

    Total number of utensils = 1271

5. Time needed = (2/4)(6 hrs.) = 3 hrs. Note that the number of inmates varies inversely with the time needed.

6. 240 - 120 - 25 = 95 inmates in their cells

7. 254 - 12 - 113 - 3 = 126 present at 10:45 AM

8. 242 - 116 - 36 - 78 + 115 = 127 present at 10:15 AM

9. Percent increase $(\dfrac{\$50}{\$400})(100) = 12\dfrac{1}{2}\%$

10. 1/2-1/3=1/6 have served between 10 and 15 years

11. 1-1/4-1/6-1/3=1/4 of all inmates are housed on the 3rd floor. Number of inmates on all floors = 90 ÷ 1/4 = 360

12. 7000 ÷ 500 = 14 inmates needed

13. The best grouping is 4 groups of 13 and 1 group of 14.

14. 1 - 1/2 - 1/5 = 3/10 and (3/10)(100) = 30

15. 250 - 200 - 12 - 17 = 21 more inmates

16. (.10)(.15) = .015 = 1.5% sentenced for more than 3 years

17. $(1100)(.15)(.80)(2/5) = 52.8 \approx 53$

18. During the 1st half-hour, 25 cartons have been packed. The number of additional hours needed = 475 ÷ (50+45) = 5. Total time = 5 1/2 hrs.

19. (36)(22) = 792 officer-days. Then, 792 ÷ 12 days = 66 officers

20. Number of court attendants in 2007 = 529 - 34 = 495

    Number of supervisors in 2007 = 2180 - 495 - 1226 - 38 = 421, closest to 425

21. % increase for correction officers, court attendants, deputy sheriffs, and supervisors =

    $=\dfrac{121}{1226} \times 100, \dfrac{34}{495} \times 100, \dfrac{2}{38} \times 100,$ and $\dfrac{77}{421} \times 100,$ respectively, which becomes (approx.) 9.9%, 6.9%, 5.3%, and 18.3%. The group with the largest percent increase is supervisors. (Note: Number of supervisors in 1988 is 498)

22. 1347 : (2414-1347) = 1347 : 1067 ≈ 1.26:1, closest to 1:1

23. $\dfrac{\$80}{\$640} = \dfrac{1}{8} = 12\dfrac{1}{2}\%$ increase

24. 1 - 1/2 = 1/2 have served fewer than 10 years. Then, (150)(1/2) = 75. 1/3 of 150 = 50 more than 15 yrs. 150 - (75+50) = 25 remaining (assuming each group is mutually exclusive)

25. 140 - 65 = 75 mph

TEST 2

DIRECTIONS: Each question or incomplete statement is followed by several suggested answers or completions. Select the one that BEST answers the question or completes the statement. *PRINT THE LETTER OF THE CORRECT ANSWER IN THE SPACE AT THE RIGHT.*

1. An investigator uses Forms A, B, and C in filling out his investigation reports. He uses Form B five times as often as Form A, and he uses Form C three times as often as Form If the total number of all forms used by the investigator in a month equals 735, how many times was Form B used?

   A.   150   B.   175   C.   205   D.   235

1.____

2. Of all the investigators in one agency, 25% work in a particular building. Of these, 12% have desks on the 14th floor.
   What percentage of the investigators work in this building but do NOT have desks on the 14th floor?

   A.   12%   B.   13%   C.   22%   D.   23%

2.____

3. An investigator is given 2 reports to read. Report P is 160 pages long and takes the investigator 3 hours and 20 minutes to read.
   If Report S is 264 pages long and the investigator reads it at the same rate as he reads Report P, how long will it take him to read Report S?
   _____ hours _____ minutes.

   A.   4; 15   B.   4; 50   C.   5; 10   D.   5; 30

3.____

4. A team of 6 investigators was assigned to interview 234 people.
   If half the investigators conduct twice as many interviews as the other half, and the slow group interviews 12 persons a day, how many days would it take to complete this assignment?
   _____ days.

   A.   4 1/4   B.   5   C.   6   D.   6 1/2

4.____

5. The investigators in one agency conduct an average of 12 interviews an hour from 10 M. to 12 Noon and from 1 P.M. to 5 P.M. daily. The director of this agency knows from past experience that 20% of those called in to be interviewed are unable to keep the appointments that were scheduled.
   If the director wants his staff to be kept occupied with interviews for the entire time period that has been set aside for this function, how many appointments should be scheduled for each day?

   A.   86   B.   90   C.   96   D.   101

5.____

6. An investigator has a 430-page report to read. The first day he is able to read 20 pages. The second day he reads 10 pages more than the first day, and the third day he reads 15 pages more than the second day.
   If on the following days he continues to read at the same rate he was reading on the third day, he will COMPLETE the report on the _____ day.

   A.   7th   B.   8th   C.   10th   D.   11th

6.____

7. The 36 investigators in an agency are each required to submit 25 investigation reports a week. These reports are filled out on a certain form, and only one copy of the form is needed per report.
Allowing 20% for wastage, how many packages of 45 forms a piece should be ordered for each weekly period?

    A. 15   B. 20   C. 25   D. 30

7.____

8. During the month, an investigative unit received $260 for stationery and telephone expenditures. It spent 43% for stationery and 1/3 of the balance for telephone service. The amount of money that was left at the end of the month was MOST NEARLY

    A. $49   B. $50   C. $99   D. $109

8.____

9. Suppose a badly cracked sidewalk, 160 feet long and 14 feet wide, is to be torn up and replaced in four equal sections.
Each section will measure _____ square feet.

    A. 40   B. 220   C. 560   D. 680

9.____

10. A businessman pays R dollars a month in rent, has a weekly payroll of P dollars, and a utility bill of U dollars for each two months.
His annual expenses can be expressed by

    A. 12(R+P+U)   B. 52(R+P+U)
    C. 12 R+52P+6U   D. 12(R+4P+2U)

10.____

11. An interviewer can interview P number of people in H number of hours, including the time needed to prepare a report on each interview.
The number of people he can interview in a work week of W hours is represented by

    A. HW/p   B. PW/H   C. PH/W   D. 35H/p

11.____

12. Claims investigated by a certain unit total $8,430,000 for the year.
If the cost of investigating these claims is 17.3 cents per $100, the yearly cost of investigating these claims is MOST NEARLY

    A. $1,450   B. $14,500   C. $145,000   D. $1,450,000

12.____

13. Suppose that a certain agency had a 2005 budget of $1,100,500. The 2006 budget was 7% higher than that of 2005, and the 2007 budget was 8% higher than that of 2006.
Of the following, which one is MOST NEARLY that agency's budget for 2007?

    A. $1,117,624   B. $1,261,737
    C. $1,265,575   D. $1,271,738

13.____

14. Suppose that on a scaled drawing of an office building floor, 1/2 inch represents three feet of actual floor dimensions.
A floor which is, in fact, 75 feet wide and 132 feet long has which of the following dimensions on this scaled drawing?
_____ inches wide and _____ inches long.

    A. 9.5; 20.5   B. 12.5; 22
    C. 17; 32   D. 25; 44

14.____

15. In 2009, the number of investigations completed in a certain unit had increased 230 over   15.____
the number completed in 2008, an increase of 10%. In 2010, the number completed
decreased 10% from the number completed in 2009. Therefore, the number of investigations completed in 2010 was _____ the number completed in 2008.

    A.   23 less than   B.   123 less than
    C.   230 more than   D.   the same as

16. Assume that during a certain period Unit A investigated 400 cases and Unit B investi-   16.____
gated 300 cases.
If each unit doubled its number of investigations, the proportion of Unit A's investigations to Unit B's investigations would then be _____ it was.

    A.   twice what   B.   one-half as large as
    C.   one-third larger than   D.   the same as

17. In a certain family, the teenage daughter's annual earnings are 5/8 the earnings of her   17.____
brother and 1/5 the earnings of her father.
If her brother earns $19,200 a year, then her father's annual earnings are

    A. $60,000   B. $75,000   C. $80,000   D. $96,000

18. Assume that, of the 1,700 verifications made by a certain investigating unit in a one week   18.____
period, 40% were birth records, 30% were military records, 10% were citizenship
records, and the remainder were miscellaneous records. Then the MOST accurate of the
following statements about the relative number of different records is that

    A.   citizenship records verifications equaled 20% of military record verifications
    B.   fewer than 700 verifications were birth records
    C.   miscellaneous records verifications were 20% more than citizenship records verifi-
        cations
    D.   more than 550 verifications were military records

19. Two units, A and B, answer respectively 1,000 and 1,500 inquiries a month.   19.____
Assuming that the number of inquiries answered by Unit A increase at the rate of 20
each month, while those answered by Unit B decrease at the rate of 5 each month, the
two units will answer the same number of inquiries at the end of _____ months.

    A.   10   B.   15   C.   20   D.   25

20. Assume that the XYZ Company has $10,402.72 cash on hand. If it pays $699.83 of this   20.____
for rent, the amount of cash on hand would be

    A. $9,792.89   B. $9,702.89   C. $9,692.89   D. $9,602.89

21. On January 31, Mr. Warren's checking account had a balance of $933.68.   21.____
If he deposited $36.40 on February 2, $126.00 on February 9, and $90.02 on February
16 and wrote no checks during this period, what was the balance of his account on
February 17?

    A. $680.26   B. $681.26   C. $1,186.10   D. $1,187.00

22. If the city department of purchase bought 190 calculators for $79.35 each and 208 calculators for $83.99 each, the TOTAL price paid for these calculators is

    A. $31,581.30   B. $32,546.42
    C. $33,427.82   D. $33,586.30

22.____

23. Subtract: 95,432
             67,596

    A. 27,836   B. 27,846   C. 27,936   D. 27,946

23.____

24. Add: $1/2 + 5/7 =$

    A. 1 3/14   B. 1 2/7   C. 1 5/14   D. 1 3/7

24.____

25. Suppose that an employee's monthly pension benefit is computed by dividing 3/5 of his final year's salary by 12. If an employee retires after earning $19,000 in his final year, his monthly pension benefit will be

    A. $840   B. $850   C. $890   D. $950

25.____

KEY (CORRECT ANSWERS)

1.	B	11.	B
2.	C	12.	B
3.	D	13.	D
4.	D	14.	B
5.	B	15.	A
6.	D	16.	D
7.	C	17.	A
8.	C	18.	B
9.	C	19.	C
10.	C	20.	B

21.	C
22.	B
23.	A
24.	A
25.	D

SOLUTIONS TO PROBLEMS

1. Let x = number of times using Form B; 1/5x = number of times using Form A; 3x = number of times using Form C. Then, 1/5x + x + 3x = 735. Solving, x = 175

2. (.25)(1-.12) = 22% work in this building but do not have desks on the 14th floor.

3. 160 pgs/200 min. = .8 page per minute. Then, 264/.8 = 330 min. = 5 hrs. 30 min.

4. 3 investigators interview 12 people per day while the other 3 investigators interview 24 people per day. Finally, 234 ÷ (12+24) = 6 1/2 days

5. Number of appointments = (12)(2+4)/.80 = 90

6. Let x = number of days in which he can read at the same rate as that on the 3rd day. We have: 1st day = 20 pgs., 2nd day = 30 pgs., 3rd day = 45 pgs. Then, 20 + 30_+ 45x = 430. Solving, x = 8.$\overline{4}$. Finally, he will need 8.$\overline{4}$ + 2 = 10.$\overline{4}$ days to complete the reading, i.e., the 11th day.

7. (36)(25) = 900 forms with no waste. Allowing for a 20% waste factor, 900 ÷ .80 = 1125 forms will be needed. Number of packages needed = 1125 ÷ 45 = 25

8. 43% was spent for stationery, and (1/3)(57%) = 19% was spent for telephone service. Amount left = (1-.43-.19)($260) = $98.80 ≈ $99

9. (160 ft.)(14 ft.)/4 = 560 sq.ft.

10. Annual expenses = 12R + 52P + 6U

11. Let x = number of people interviewed in W hrs. Then, $\frac{P}{H} = \frac{X}{W}$ Solving, x = PW/H

12. $8,430,000 ÷ $100 = 84,300. Then, (84,300)(.173) = $14,583.90, which is closest to $14,500 in the selections.

13. Budget for 2007 = ($1,100,500)(1.07)(1.08) ≈ $1,271,738

14. (75/3)(1/2") = 12.5" wide, and (132/3)(1/2") = 22" long

15. Number of investigations in 2008 = 230 ÷ 10% = 2300
Number of investigations in 2009 = 2300 + 230 = 2530
Number of investigations in 2010 = (2530X.90) = 2277
Finally, 2277 represents 23 less than 2300.

16. New numbers would be 800 and 600 for Units A and B, respectively. Then, 800/600 = 4:3 = 400/300. The new ratio equals the old ratio.

17. Daughter's earnings = (5/8) ($19,200) = $12,000. Then, the father's earnings = $12,000 ÷ 1/5 = $60,000

18. (.40)(1700) = 680 birth records, which is less than 700.

19. Let x = number of months. Then, 1000 + 20x = 1500 - 5x Solving, x = 20

20. $10,402.72 - $699.83 = $9702.89

21. $933.68 + $36.40 + $126.00 + $90.02 = $1186.10

22. (190)($79.35) + (208)($83 .99) = $32,546.42

23. 95,432 - 67,596 = 27,836

24. 1/2 + 5/7 = 7/14 + 10/14 = 17/14 = 1 3/14

25. Monthly pension benefit = (3/5) ($19,000) ÷ 12 = $950

TEST 3

DIRECTIONS: Each question or incomplete statement is followed by several suggested answers or completions. Select the one that BEST answers the question or completes the statement. *PRINT THE LETTER OF THE CORRECT ANSWER IN THE SPACE AT THE RIGHT.*

1. A certain store is selling cloth table napkins. The small size costs 35¢ each or 99¢ for a package of 3. The large size costs 55¢ each or $1.59 for a package of 3.
   The LOWEST possible price for 11 large napkins and 10 small ones is   1.____

   A. $4.03   B. $8.99   C. $9.19   D. $11.13

2. Children's sweaters were sold in a certain store for $13.95 each. They were then placed on sale at 40% off.   2.____
   If a woman bought 3 sweaters on sale and was charged $24.11 (excluding sales tax), she was

   A. charged the correct price
   B. overcharged $7.37
   C. undercharged $1.00
   D. undercharged $17.74

3. Assume you check the weight of all the packages of meat in a certain supermarket. Of the 585 packages tested, 40% are shortweight. Of the shortweight packages, 15% are shortweight by 10% or more.   3.____
   The number of packages of meat that are shortweight by 10% or more is MOST NEARLY

   A. 22   B. 23   C. 35   D. 52

4. A certain car rental agency charges $27.00 a day and 30¢ a mile, but gives a 15% discount to anyone renting a car for 1 week or more.   4.____
   If one man rents a car for 3 days and drives 375 miles, and another man rents a car for 9 days and drives 775 miles, the total cost for the two rentals will be MOST NEARLY

   A. $234.84   B. $597.00   C. $605.10   D. $669.00

5. Of the 435 boxes of Brand X cookies on the shelves in a certain supermarket, 31% are more than 5% shortweight. Of the remaining boxes, 18% weigh over 5% more than they should.   5.____
   The number of boxes that fall within 5% of the correct weight is MOST NEARLY

   A. 164   B. 213   C. 222   D. 246

6. Convert 4/9 to a decimal. Carry your work to four decimal places.   6.____

   A. .4445   B. .4455   C. .4444   D. .4454

7. Convert 1/2% to a fraction.   7.____

   A. 1/2   B. 1/200   C. 1/50   D. 1/5

8. What percent is $75 of $575. Carry your work to four decimal places.   8.____

   A. 1304   B. 13.0434   C. 13   D. 130.4

9. An invoice amounts to $1,875 less 10% and 10%; terms 2/10 net 30. It is paid within the discount period.
What is the NET amount of the check?

9._____

    A. $1,488.38   B. $1,488.37   C. $1,500   D. $1,470

10. The Bon Bon Company buys candy at $1.60 a pound.
At what price per pound should candy be marked in order to sell at a discount of 20% from the marked price and still make a profit of 20% on the selling price?

10._____

    A. $2.50   B. $2.60   C. $2.70   D. $2.80

11. A washing machine and a dishwashing machine were sold for $240 each. The clothes washer was sold at a loss of 25% of cost, and the dishwasher at a gain of 25% of cost.
How much was gained or lost on the entire transaction, or did the dealer break even?

11._____

    A. $32 loss   B. $20 gain
    C. $48 gain   D. No gain or loss

12. Three pipes fill a pool of water. One pipe can fill it alone in 6 hours, another in 8 hours, and a third in 12 hours.
How many hours will be used to fill the pool if all pipes are opened at the same time?

12._____

    A. 8 2/3   B. 2 2/3   C. 26   D. 7 1/3

13. If 10 men working 8 hours a day can do a job in 3 days, how many days are needed if 6 men work 10 hours a day?

13._____

    A. 4   B. 5   C. 3 1/2   D. 5 1/2

14. The Dunn Company gave each employee a bonus to be determined as follows: 15% on that part of his salary which is $30,000 or less, 10% on that part of his salary greater than $30,000 and up to and including $60,000, 5% on that part of his salary over $60,000. Mr. Smith, an employee, received a bonus of $8,250. Find his basic salary.

14._____

    A. $37,500   B. $47,500   C. $62,500   D. $75,000

15. A freight train leaves New York for Buffalo at 9:00 P.M. and travels at the rate of 30 miles an hour. At 12:00 Midnight of the same day, on the same railroad, a passenger train leaves New York for Buffalo and travels at 54 miles an hour.
The passenger train will overtake the freight train at APPROXIMATELY _____ A.M.

15._____

    A. 6:45   B. 3:22   C. 3:45   D. 4:54

16. A salesman gets a commission of 6% on his sales.
If he wants his commission to amount to $720, he will have to sell merchandise totaling

16._____

    A. $1,420   B. $12,000   C. $1,200   D. $120

17. A merchant purchased a suit for $240.00 and sold it for $320.00.
The mark-up on the cost price is

17._____

    A. 25%   B. 33 1/3%   C. 75%   D. 15%

18. Assume that out of a shipment of 135 crates of oranges, 11 crates of oranges do not meet acceptable standards. The percentage of crates of oranges which meet acceptable standards is MOST NEARLY

    A. 8.1%   B. 12.3%   C. 87.7%   D. 91.9%

18.____

19. Assume that a shipment of 35 cases of goods, each containing 72 packages, is to be returned to the manufacturer if more than 3% of the packages prove to be defective. The maximum number of defective packages the shipment may contain in order for it NOT to be rejected is

    A. 74   B. 75
    C. 76   D. none of the above

19.____

20. Assume that two shipments of goods arrive at a warehouse. The first shipment contains 280 boxes, each measuring 4" x 8" x 10". The second shipment contains 94 cartons, each measuring 1' x 1' x 4'.
The total number of cubic feet required to store both shipments is MOST NEARLY

    A. 428   B. 466   C. 804   D. 992

20.____

21. Assume that an agency uses 700 reams of bond paper per month and that it must have a three-month supply of bond paper on hand at all times. It takes 2 1/2 months from the time a supply of bond paper is ordered to the time it is delivered.
What is the MINIMUM re-order point?

    A. 800   B. 1,750   C. 3,100   D. 3,850

21.____

22. A dietician wishes to order enough butter to serve 2,300 school children at lunch time. 15% of the children will take two pats of butter; 10% of the children will take no butter; the remainder will take one pat of butter. Each pat of butter weighs 3/16 of an ounce. APPROXIMATELY how many pounds of butter should the dietician order? (Allow no butter for wastage.)

    A. 16   B. 29   C. 35   D. 41

22.____

23. By taking advantage of a series discount of 4%, 3%, and 2%, respectively, a buyer paid $7.17 less than list price for an article.
The list price of the article was MOST NEARLY

    A. $78   B. $79   C. $81   D. $82

23.____

24. 572 divided by .52 is

    A. 1100   B. 110   C. 11.10   D. 11.00

24.____

25. The number of decimal places in the product of 0.4266 and 0.3333 is

    A. 8   B. 6   C. 4   D. 2

25.____

KEY (CORRECT ANSWERS)

1.	C	11.	A
2.	C	12.	B
3.	C	13.	A
4.	B	14.	D
5.	D	15.	C
6.	C	16.	B
7.	B	17.	B
8.	B	18.	D
9.	C	19.	B
10.	A	20.	A

21.	D
22.	B
23.	D
24.	A
25.	A

SOLUTIONS TO PROBLEMS

1. 11 large napkins cost (3)($1.59) + (2)(.55) = $5.87

   10 small napkins cost (3)(.99) + (1)(.35) = $3.32

   Total minimum cost = $9.19

2. On sale, the cost of 3 sweaters = (3)($13.95)(.60) = $25.11 Therefore, this woman was undercharged $1.00

3. (585)(.40)(.15) = 35.1 ≈ 35

4. Cost for 1st man = (3)($27.00) + (375)(.30) = $193.50

   Cost for 2nd man = [(9)($27.00)+(775)(.30)](.85) = $404.18 Total cost = $597.68, which is closest to $597.00 among the selections.

5. (435)(.31) ≈ 135 more than 5% shortweight. Also, of the remaining 300 boxes, (.18)(300) = 54 are more than 5% overweight. Thus, 435 - 135 - 54 = 246 fall within 5% of the correct weight.

6. $4/9 = .\overline{4} = .4444$

7. 1/2% = 1/2·1/100 = 1/200

8. $\dfrac{\$75}{\$575} = \dfrac{3}{23} \approx 13.04\%$

9. ($1875)(.90)(.90) = $1518.75, which is closest to $1500 among the selections

10. Let x = marked price. Then, x - .20x = selling price. So, x - .20x - $1.60 = .20(x-.20x). Simplifying this equation, .80x - 1.60 = .20x - .04x. Solving, x = $2.50

11. Total selling price = (2)(240) = $480. Cost of clothes washer = $240 ÷ .75 = $320, and the cost of dishwasher = $240 ÷ 1.25 = $192. Total cost of these 2 items = $512, so that the loss = $512 - $480 = $32

12. Let x = number of hours. Then, (1/6)(x) + (1/8)(x) + (1/12x) = 1 Simplifying, 3/8x = 1. Solving, x = 2 2/3

13. (10)(8)(3) = 240 man-hours. Then, 240 ÷ 6 ÷ 10 = 4 days

14. If his salary were $30,000, his bonus = ($30,000)(.15) = $4500. If his salary were $60,000, his bonus = $4500 + (.10)($60,000-$30,000) = $7500. Thus, his salary exceeds $60,000. His bonus of $8250 exceeds $7500 by $750. If x = his basic salary, then (.05)(x-$60,000) = $750. Solving, x = $75,000

15. Let x = number of hours of travel for the passenger train. Then, 30(x+3) = 54x. Solving, x = 3.75 = 3 hrs. 45 min. The actual time is 3:45 AM.

16. $720 ÷ .06 = $12,000 worth of merchandise

17. $80/$240 = 33 1/3%

18. 124/135 ≈ 91.9%

19. (35)(72)(.03) = 75.6. So, 75 would be the highest allowable number of defectives.

20. (280)(4/12)(8/12)(10/12) + (94)(1)(1)(4) ≈ 428 cu.ft.

21. (700)(3+2 1/2) = 3850 reams

22. Number of pats needed = (2300)(.15)(2) + (2300)(.75)(1) = 2415. Number of ounces = (2415)(3/16) ≈ 453. Finally, number of pounds = 453 ÷ 16 ≈ 28

23. Let x = list price. Then, x - (x)(.96)(.97)(.98) = $7.17 Solving, x ≈ $82

24. 572 ÷ .52 = 1100

25. (.4266)(.3333) = an answer with 8 decimal places.
     Actual answer = .14218578

———————

Made in the USA
Las Vegas, NV
25 January 2025

16914076R00118